The Naked Public Square Reconsidered

AMERICAN IDEALS AND INSTITUTIONS SERIES

Robert P. George, series editor

Published in partnership with the James Madison Program in American Ideals and Institutions at Princeton University, this series is dedicated to the exploration of enduring questions of political thought and constitutional law; to the promotion of the canon of the Western intellectual tradition as it nourishes and informs contemporary politics; and to the application of foundational Western principles to modern social problems.

The Naked Public Square Reconsidered

Religion and Politics in the
Twenty-First Century

Edited by Christopher Wolfe

Wilmington, Delaware

The naked public square reconsidered : religion and politics in the
twenty-first century / edited by Christopher Wolfe. —1st ed.—Wilmington, Del. : ISI Books, c2009.

    p. ; cm.
(American ideals and institutions series)

    ISBN: 978-1-935191-27-8 (cloth)
    A reconsideration of "The naked public square: religion and
democracy in America" by Richard John Neuhaus, published in
1984.
    Includes bibliographical references and index.

    1. United States—Religion—21st century. 2. United States—
Moral conditions. 3. Religion and politics—United States—21st
century. 4. United States—Politics and government—21st century. I.
Wolfe, Christopher. II. Neuhaus, Richard John. Naked public square.
III. Title. IV. Title: Religion and politics in the twenty-first century.
V. Series.

BL2525 .N35 2009   2008940176
261.7/09730905—dc22   0907

                    ISI Books
            Intercollegiate Studies Institute
                3901 Centerville Road
             Wilmington, DE 19807-1938
                  www.isibooks.org

        Manufactured in the United States of America

Contents

Foreword:
A Tribute to Richard John Neuhaus

Robert P. George

In the early 1970s, Lutheran pastor Richard John Neuhaus was poised to become the nation's next great liberal public intellectual—the Reinhold Niebuhr of his generation. He had going for him everything he needed to be not merely accepted but lionized by the liberal establishment. First, of course, there were his natural gifts as a thinker, writer, and speaker. Then there was a set of left-liberal credentials that were second to none. He had been an outspoken and prominent civil rights campaigner, indeed, someone who had marched literally arm-in-arm with his friend Martin Luther King. He had founded one of the most visible anti–Vietnam War organizations. He moved easily in elite circles and was regarded by everyone as a "right-thinking" (i.e., left-thinking) intellectual-activist operating within the world of mainline Protestant religion.

But Father Richard John Neuhaus did not go through life, as it once seemed he would, collecting honorary degrees from the most prestigious universities, giving warmly received speeches before major professional associations and at international congresses of the great and the good, being a celebrated guest at social and political gatherings on the Upper West Side, or appearing on the Sunday network news shows as spiritual guarantor of the moral validity of liberalism's favored policies and practices.

The reason for this is that something happened: abortion. It became something it had never been before, namely, a contentious issue in American culture and politics. Neuhaus opposed abortion for the same reasons he had fought for civil rights and against the Vietnam War. At the root of his thinking was the conviction that human beings, as creatures fashioned in the image and likeness of God, possess a profound, inherent, and equal dignity. This dignity must be respected by all and protected by law. That, so far as Neuhaus was concerned, was not only a Biblical mandate but also the bedrock principle of the American constitutional order. Respect for the dignity of human beings meant, among other things, not subjecting them to a system of racial oppression; not wasting their lives in futile wars; not slaughtering them in the womb.

While many other liberals deserted the cause of life, Richard Neuhaus stood by his convictions and refused to yield. As Father Neuhaus's great friend, and fellow Lutheran convert to Catholicism, Father Leonard Klein, put it in a beautiful tribute, "Richard's politics changed precisely because his principles did not change." His profound commitment to the sanctity of human life in all stages and conditions placed him on a different path, one that led him out of the liberal fold and into intense opposition. As a kind of artifact of his youth, he remained to the end a registered member of the Democratic Party. But he stood defiantly against many of the doctrines and policies that came to define that party in his lifetime, among which was the modern separationist view that would drive religion from the public square. He was, in fact, their most forceful and effective critic— the scourge of the post-'60s liberals. He was not, as things turned out, their Niebuhr, but their nemesis.

On some issues, Neuhaus's political views shifted because he came to doubt the wisdom and efficacy of programs and policies he had once believed in. The liberal movement's capitulation to the abortion license and the conservative movement's resolution to fight it opened him up to a reconsideration of where he should be—which for him meant a reconsideration of where the truth was to be found—on a variety of questions. He grew more skeptical of the bureaucratized big-government programs by which liberals sought to fight poverty and other social ills. He began to see that most of these programs were not only ineffective, but counterproductive. For a variety of reasons, statist solutions to poverty tended to increase and entrench rather than diminish it. And not unrelatedly, governmental expansion tended to weaken the institutions of civil society, above all the family and the church, on which we rely for the formation of decent, honest, responsible, civic-minded, law-abiding citizens—citizens capable of caring for themselves, their families, and people in need.

With respect to the subject of this volume, Neuhaus famously fought the liberal movement as it increasingly associated itself with the cause of driving religion and religiously informed moral witness out of the public square and into the merely private domain. His book *The Naked Public Square* did far more than introduce a catchy phrase; it revolutionized the debate. Neuhaus easily saw through the dubious (and sometimes laughable) "interpretations" of the religion clause of the First Amendment by which ACLU lawyers and judges in their ideological thrall attempted to privatize religion and marginalize people of faith. What motivated him most strongly, however, was the perception of the indispensable roles played by religious institutions and other mediating structures in preserving a regime of ordered liberty against unjustified encroachments by the administrative apparatus of the state. The real danger, as Neuhaus rightly saw it, was not that religious groups would seize control of the state and establish a theocracy; it was that the state would undermine the autonomy and standing of those structures that provide credible sources of authority in people's lives beyond the authority of the state—structures that could, when necessary, prophetically challenge unjust or overweening state power.

For Neuhaus, the liberal movement had gone wrong not only on the sanctity of human life, but on the range of issues on which it had succumbed to the ideology of the post-1960s cultural Left. While celebrating "personal liberation," "diverse lifestyles," "self-expression," and "if it feels good, do it," all in the name of respecting "the individual," liberalism had gone hook, line, and sinker for a set of doctrines and social policies that would only increase the size and enhance the control of the state—mainly by enervating the only institutions available to provide counter-weights to state power.

As a veteran of the civil rights movement, Neuhaus knew just how effective religious institutions could be in speaking truth to power and challenging unjust laws and policies. Of course, liberals did not complain about religious witness in the public square when what was being witnessed to was a cause they believed in, such as ending racial segregation. But when religious people began speaking out in defense of the child in the womb, many liberals suddenly decided that the constitutional principle of religious nonestablishment required the privatization of religion and the marginalization of religious voices in discourse and deliberation about law and public policy. Knowing a double standard when he saw one, Neuhaus immediately and loudly cried "foul!"

As Neuhaus never tired of observing, our goal should not be to replace the *naked* public square with the *sacred* public square. Because he believed profoundly in religious liberty, political equality, and participatory democracy, he was as opposed to the establishment of religion as he was to the establishment of the pseudo-religion of liberal secularism. He loathed both theocracy and its secularist equivalent. Neuhaus's vision, and that, as he rightly thought, of our nation's Founders, was the *civil* public square in which all voices are welcome and all citizens—be they Catholics or Protestants, Christians or Jews, Muslims, Hindus, members of other faiths, and those of no religious faith at all—are free to make their arguments and vie for the allegiance of their fellow citizens. In the *civil* public square, people participate in democracy not as "unencumbered selves" (to use Michael Sandel's apt phrase), but as citizens who draw on the wisdom, as best they understand it, of the many traditions represented among them in an effort to order their lives together justly and pursue the common good.

Neuhaus was a fierce critic of the ideology of "strict separationism" by which secularists and other liberals sought to use raw judicial power to effectively disenfranchise people of faith who reject liberal orthodoxies. He fully accepted, however, the separation of church and state. He did not believe in a "Christian America" in anything more than a sociological sense (the overwhelming majority of Americans are Christians), and he adamantly insisted on the separation of the institutions of the church from the institutions of the state. He believed that the state should not tell religious communities how to run their affairs, and he believed equally strongly that religious institutions should not control the levers of government. His central message was that the separation of church and state should never be twisted to mean the separation of religion and religiously informed moral witness from public life. The message was no invention of his: he learned from teachers such as Rabbi Abraham Joshua Heschel and the Reverend Martin Luther King.

This volume commemorates the publication of *The Naked Public Square* in the best way possible: it carries on and develops the themes of the conversation in which he was such an active and eloquent participant. Its prominent contributors disagree on various points, but, happily, they all share his deep commitment to the civil public square.

Introduction

Christopher Wolfe

Richard John Neuhaus was one of the most influential com-mentators on religion, politics, and culture in the past three decades. He established the influential journal *First Things*, built it into a source of serious intellectual exchanges, and used it as a "bully pulpit" to comment monthly on a wide range of issues and events. Overlapping his work at *First Things* was his con-stant, and remarkably successful, effort to form alliances or at least promote vibrant conversation among significant figures from a variety of different faiths, with "Evangelicals and Catho-lics Together" being perhaps his most notable achievement. But the one thing he may most be remembered for was changing the framework of the debate on religion and politics questions, with the publication in 1984 of *The Naked Public Square*.

While there have always been certain tensions in America regard-ing the relationship between religion and politics, until relatively recently in our history these tensions have concerned *what* role religion should play in our national life and what sort of religion it ought to be that was playing this role. Only in the second half of the twentieth century did the question become *whether* religion as such had any role to play in American politics.

The U.S. Supreme Court's 1947 ruling in *Everson v. Board of Education* symbolized the rise of this new question when it argued that the government should be neutral not just between religions, but between religion and nonreligion. Yet *Everson* itself accommodated religion to some extent by permitting public support for transportation to religiously affiliated schools. Even after *Everson*, the Court could say, in Justice William O. Douglas's famous phrase in *Zorach v. Clauson*, that our "political institutions presuppose a Supreme Being."

It was the Warren Court, in the tumultuous 1960s, that worked out the implications of *Everson* more thoroughly, especially in its decisions striking down prayer in public schools, in *Engel v. Vitale* and *Abington School District v. Schempp*. Together with the abortion decision in *Roe v. Wade*, these cases represented an important dimension of the modern "culture wars." Conservative Protestants, in particular, took these decisions as an assault on the traditional benevolent accommodation of religion in American national life and began to mobilize politically in response during the 1970s. By the beginning of the 1980s, America was divided into deeply hostile camps on questions of religion and politics.

Richard John Neuhaus's *The Naked Public Square* appeared in this context in 1984, and its metaphor quickly came to symbolize the reaction against the secularization of American public life. The public square had been denuded of anything other than purely value-neutral references to religion, or, at least it could be said, that seemed to be the goal of the most powerful intellectual forces in the United States, who were receiving a sympathetic hearing at the Supreme Court. Opponents of this trend were very much on the defensive. Many of them responded that America was a "Christian nation" and couched their arguments in the largely biblical terms they felt most comfortable using—arguments that seemed to their antagonists to beg the question. Neuhaus's book provided a sophisticated intellectual response, deeply grounded in history, political philosophy, and theology, and it is no surprise, therefore, that it provided a rallying point for those who wished to restore religion to public life without creating the dangerous union of church and state that had been the object of the leading American Founders to prevent. The image of the "naked public square" became the effective rhetorical counter to the "wall of separation" metaphor of strict separationists.

As the book was published, the Supreme Court was already backing off its apparent move toward strict separationism in certain ways. While the course of its decisions was widely regarded as erratic and unprincipled and satisfied no one, it could at least be said that the Court was attempting to give something to each side in the dispute. While strongly reaffirming its secularist public school prayer decisions, for example, it began to allow more space for government aid to religiously affiliated schools, and it tolerated various forms of public religious symbolism, including publicly sponsored nativity scenes (in appropriately diluted contexts) and state legislative invocations.

In addition to court cases, disputes about religion and politics have also arisen in broader political contexts, as, for example, regarding George W. Bush's "faith-based initiative" and state and local battles regarding evolution and creationism and intelligent design in the public schools. Questions were also raised in the context of American foreign policy, especially as foreign policy elites (both in the United States and abroad) worried that President Bush was adopting a religiously inspired version of America's role in the world.

In the early twenty-first century, it seems that the culture wars continue in the United States in the famed "red state/blue state" divide. Religion continues to be an important element in those divisions, with more conservative and active religious believers gravitating toward the Republican Party, and secularists tending toward the Democratic Party. (The political split along religious lines led to satiric proposals after the 2000 election that the blue states secede and join Canada, creating the United States of Canada, and leaving the rest of the [red] states as "Jesusland."[1])

The continuing importance of religion in the public square and Democratic Party losses in 2000 and 2004 even led notable Democratic Party figures (such as Barack Obama) to suggest that the party's electoral fortunes depended on erasing the impression that the party is hostile to religion.

Disputes regarding the proper relation between religion and politics also continue to have a significant place in contemporary political theory. Questions about religiously based arguments in *public reason* and questions regarding democratic citizenship and education have been subjects of considerable discussion. John Rawls's depiction of a *public reason* requirement for public discourse struck some as an effort to persuade religious believers to embrace "political liberalism," while at the same time marginalizing or privatizing religion, which was seen as a permanent source of political divisiveness and a threat to public peace.[2] Amy Guttmann's *Democratic Education*,[3] James Dwyer's *Religious Schools v. Children's Rights*,[4] and Stephen Macedo's *Diversity and Distrust*[5] were examples of books that focused heavily on the potential incompatibility between the requirements and goals of liberal democracy (especially education in a liberal democracy) and traditional religious views.

Given the continuing and intense debate about religion and politics in both practical and theoretical arenas, a reexamination of the issues raised by *The Naked Public Square* in light of events of subsequent decades seems eminently desirable. The contributors to this volume, drawn from different parts of the political spectrum, offer us some valuable reflections on the subject.

Gerard Bradley begins the book with what some "accommodationists" might consider a surprisingly optimistic argument: the "privatization" project of the Supreme Court has been in decay for the past two decades or so and may soon be rejected entirely. Initiated in 1962 with the school prayer decision in *Engel v. Vitale*, the judicial project of creating an extreme separation of church and state reached its zenith in 1984 and began to go downhill thereafter. This shift occurred largely because the hysterical fears underlying the 1984–85 cases have disappeared. In the recent *Newdow* case, Justice Sandra Day O'Connor's opinion (an opinion on the merits, unlike the Court's opinion) even flirts with upholding the Pledge of Allegiance as a living affirmation of some propositions about God, Providence, and America today, though she can't quite give up her commitment to the naked public square. But an appropriate understanding of the "metaphysics of liberty" would, in fact, justify state affirmation of such propositions.

Mary Ann Glendon takes a decidedly less optimistic position. In the first part of her essay, she analyzes the effects of Neuhaus's book twenty-five years after its publication. She is particularly interested in two of the facts he highlights: the growing tendency to exclude religiously grounded moral viewpoints from public life, and the danger that an overzealous secularization program poses to the cultural foundations of the republic.

Regarding the first question, Glendon argues that since 1984 the situation has in general become worse. Thus, although the decisions of the U.S. Supreme Court regarding the role of religion in public life lack coherence, the decisions of the federal courts have continued to lean against public acknowledgment and accommodation of religion. As for the decisions of the local legislatures, Neuhaus's ideas have met a warmer reception, and many decisions taken in the past twenty years by these local legislatures have been in the direction of his recommendations.

In the last part of the essay, Glendon builds on Madison's argument that a republic needs citizens with a higher degree of virtue than any other form of state organization. She argues that education provided solely by the state and devoid of any religious substrate may be detrimental to the creation of virtuous citizens.

J. H. H. Weiler examines the Neuhaus thesis as it applies to the European Union, the "shared public square" of Europe. He contends that the refusal to include a reference to God and/or Christianity in the preamble of the proposed EU Constitution (and, before it, in the European Charter of Human Rights) represented not multicultural tolerance, but rather true constitutional intolerance and a betrayal of the deepest ideals of European integration and the Union. Christianity as cultus is a vehicle, manifestation, and repository of European culture. But today Europe suffers from "Christophobia"—not simply a "principled" constitutional notion of secularism but a powerful negative animus toward Christianity. Religion—the protection of which comes under the rubric of freedom of conscience—is a matter of private belief and must remain outside the public piazza. The relative weakness of the constitutional reasoning for this, contrasted with the ferocity of the opposition to any explicit reference to God or to Christianity, suggests deeper motives: a complex amalgam of fear of offending non-Christian minorities, Christian guilt, vulgar politics, hostility to controversial Church teachings, and early childhood experiences of European elites regarding religion, as well as the simple fact that too many Christians "have elected to disrobe from their glorious spiritual and cultural heritage as they enter" the public square.

Michael Pakaluk starts his analysis of the current trend of secularization with a narration of the events described by Weiler: the refusal to include the *invocatio Dei* in the preamble of the European Constitution and the famous rejection of Rocco Buttiglione as EU commissioner for his personal opposition to active homosexuality. Pakaluk argues that at the origin of this exaggerated secularism in public life is the wrong view that secularism is in fact the neutral position to take, when in fact the choice regarding the place of God in public life is a binary one: either you accept Him or you reject Him. The nonaffirmation in this case means rejection.

Pakaluk also criticizes John Rawls for arguing that when people deliberate on matters of basic justice they should not rely on any particular philosophical or metaphysical views because not everyone will share these views—which means that religious beliefs should not have a significant place in public debate. Pakaluk points out that some religious beliefs, such as the existence of God, can be interpreted as basic knowledge, and not merely as beliefs. If we know that there is God, then references to God in public discourse do not contradict the requirements of legitimate public debate, since, as Rawls himself argues, basic facts about the natural world and basic knowledge should be included.

John Finnis points out that human flourishing's basic aspects can be identified and defended without appealing to any idea of divine causality. In several of Finnis's own books, that "further question" of ultimate causality is deferred to the end of the books, partly for reasons of "economy": "the adapting of exposition to the receptiveness, the state of mind, of one's expected audience." Finnis wants to make two points here: first, that the whole course of reflection, heading toward the reasonable judgment that God exists and is relevant to understanding more adequately why our responsibilities matter, is an exercise in public reason, and second, that the argument's conclusion entails that neither atheism nor radical agnosticism is entitled to be treated as the "default" position in public reason, deliberation, and decisions.

Finnis's intent is to delineate the status of public revelation in public reason. He argues that "revelation of God's nature and intentions for us is 'public,' in the focal sense, when it is offered in public preaching attested to by signs or miracles such as resurrection, otherwise inexplicable healing, fulfillment of prophecies, and so forth"; but the evidentiary force of these is immeasurably enhanced by the further fact that the teaching is itself *morally* attractive. We use our natural understanding of the good as a criterion in judging the claims of revelation. There is a "humanly necessary interdependence of natural reason and revelation." For example, human reason can affirm equality of all men, and yet we can doubt that this principle will be "steadily understood and affirmed" without the support of revelation.

Finnis concludes by arguing that John Rawls's understanding of public reason, which requires the setting aside of comprehensive views, including religious beliefs, is "crippled by its ambiguity and unprincipled exception-making." It is ambiguous because, if it refers to ideal epistemic conditions, Rawls's criterion ("all [reasonable] people can reasonably be expected to agree") excludes nothing; but if the criterion refers to the actual prevailing epistemic state of affairs, then it again excludes nothing because Rawls accepts that reasonable people can and do hold some unreasonable views, so that there is no interestingly substantive view that *all* reasonable people agree to. It makes exceptions for secularists, who are assumed to be inside a public consensus, while arbitrarily relegating "rationalist believers" to a position outside of the consensus.

Rogers Smith agrees with Finnis's main contention that arguments from revelation in the public square should be accepted and welcomed as consistent with public reason. He goes on to raise questions, however, about four implications of the main thesis in Finnis's work. First, he claims that the public ethos should be one not of public reason but of robust democratic contestation, in which every view should be allowed on an equal basis. Thus even fascist or racist views should be allowed in the public forum. Second, religion should not be given a preference relative to secular moral outlooks. Thus, the religious should get equal public benefits, but they should not get any special treatment or any exemptions from state requirements. Third, Smith attacks the claim of the Supreme Court that although a law may legitimately be based on religious reasons, it cannot be based on religious reasons alone. Fourth, he criticizes the way in which President George W. Bush uses religious discourse in a way that does not allow for democratic contestation, seeming to assert that his actions are divinely inspired, and therefore ruling out any contestation.

Eric Gregory agrees with Finnis on two important points. First, he appreciates Finnis's (and Neuhaus's) support for the rights-based classical liberal democratic experiment, conceived primarily in terms of the constitutional rule of law. Gregory affirms, with Finnis, a sense of secularity as an essential element of Christian belief. Secularity in this sense means the shared time afforded all humanity by the common grace of God and the rejection of the sacralization of the political order. Second, he shares Finnis's and Neuhaus's concerns about efforts to exclude religion from public life and the wholesale separation of law from morality, and rejects Rawlsian public reason as "undemocratic, unrealizable, politically self-defeating, and premised on a failed epistemology."

Gregory, however, offers two lines of critical response to Finnis. The first is theological. He asks whether the state is essentially pagan; or more precisely, is the state a pagan invention that is somehow capable of making human persons less immoral, and thereby capable of securing some goods we would not otherwise have? In Finnis's account, Gregory believes, the government seems to know something about religion as a basic good, even as it remains neutral with respect to competing visions of this basic good. Thus, there seems to be a tension between his account of the state and his account of religion as a basic good. Does the state only protect religion as a basic good, or can the state ever promote it?

The second question is sociological: do we need a shared ethical *theory* to maintain a common morality? Are Finnis's arguments about the need for revelation to support the ideal of equality, for example, pragmatic and speculative—that is, psychological remarks about the sociology of group adherence to the idea of equality? Or are they to be taken in some more robust sense? Put colloquially, do you need God to justify and maintain human rights rather than the mere rights of citizens? Gregory agrees that it is hard to imagine the development of human rights discourse in the West without the Christian tradition, but he worries that Finnis is placing too much value on the need for a *shared theory* of human rights. Finnis claims that the bases for "a defense of radical equality of men and women" is found in developed Christian teaching, whereas Gregory doubts that we "need to agree on our theories of morality in order to sustain democratic practices and institutions." Religious traditions should help liberals imagine a better kind of liberalism and work to help their adherents be the sort of persons who work for justice in political communities, but such efforts do not demand recourse to an account of "basic goods" or unanimous consent on any given ethical theory. Aristotle thought that one needs a morally upright culture to become moral, but Christians should hold otherwise, relying on grace for the training, directing, correcting, healing, and even perfecting of the gift of virtue that Christians claim to find in the law of Christ.

William Galston finds a surprising similarity between Neuhaus and John Rawls: both seem to say that all public decisions must be made through arguments that are public in character. Galston believes that this argument rests on an excessive confidence in reason's power to resolve the deepest differences. As an example, he offers the differences between Orthodox Jews and conservative Christians regarding the issue of cloning. Galston states that the Judaic tradition of the Torah is at the basis of the acceptance of cloning by the Orthodox Jews. There are three teachings of the Torah relevant here: that human beings are the stewards of God's creation and therefore have the right to shape what God has given; that there are moral imperatives to cure disease and save lives; and that the moral status of the preembryo (up to forty days) is less than that of humans. Galston's conclusion, therefore, is that orthodox faiths that unite in resisting religious liberalism and modernism may disagree about the content of theology and about its social implications.

Galston concludes by defending a pluralist understanding of the relationship between faith communities and political communities. According to this understanding, faith communities should be able to request exemptions from otherwise binding public laws when these laws command what faith or conscience prohibit.

Hadley Arkes imagines giving a dinner talk on the fiftieth anniversary of *The Naked Public Square*. He points out that scholarship supported Neuhaus's argument regarding the pervasive religious understanding of the Founders as the ground for the laws they instituted. The political laws depended on the moral law, which pointed to the Author of the moral law. This understanding was nurtured in a *communal* teaching, was developed with argument and the canons of reason accessible to people, which is to say, *public reason*, and had an inescapable public significance, especially in the life of a republic.

Speaking some twenty-five years hence, Arkes "looks back" on the widening gulf of sectarianisms in the early twenty-first century—secular and religious—and imagines an increasing intolerance of traditional moral views on matters such as gay marriage. The lesson to be learned is that "the teachings and compulsions of the law move from the public realm until they spill over into the private realm as well." The right proclaimed at the top of the state, by the courts, works its way out then from the public to the private. And as this trend reaches its fullest expression, the public square becomes even more "naked" and hostile than the public square portrayed by Richard Neuhaus in his famous book. But, as he speaks in 2034, there have been signs of an emerging revival of more traditional views, even in the heart of secular universities, and, after all, for those who believe, there is always reason to hope.

Richard John Neuhaus's Afterword is the "last word" in this book, and, lamentably, it now represents a posthumous contribution to the ongoing conversation he did so much to shape. He notes that his book had the fortune to represent an increasing sense of things that had not quite been articulated. In retrospect, the book seems clearly to have been directed to the dominant liberal elites who were familiar with the intellectual history and practice of liberal democracy, asking them to understand what the emerging religious right thought they had gotten wrong. Today, conservative Christians are more active in the public sphere, and some liberals recognize that "this constitutional order is not sustainable apart from the cultural, moral, and religious expression of the self-evident truths on which it is founded." The reemergence of religious influence in public life creates a danger of imposing moral values, but debate about the legitimate limits of law is part of democratic deliberation. Neuhaus is "skeptical about the possibility of agreeing on clear rules in determining what counts as public reason," inclining toward Rogers Smith's "robust democratic contestation," in which moral reason and natural law arguments play an important part. Like Eric Gregory, he has doubts about human reason, which is corrupted—though, thankfully, not entirely so—and so "we avail ourselves of whatever reasonable arguments, popular aspirations, rational fears, and motivating visions—so long as they are not dishonest or debasing—in order to achieve a closer approximation of justice, which is the virtue most proper to politics." What matters for us is whether we have tried within the circumstances given to us.

The Naked Public Square went to the heart of the issue of religion and politics at an important moment in American life, even as it helped to change the circumstances to which it was a response. Since its publication, the public square in America has certainly become less naked in various ways, even as the dominant academic theorists of liberalism (especially Rawlsians) have fought a powerful rearguard action to sustain the momentum of an earlier Supreme Court drive for separationism and as political divisions between secularists and the religious right remain very deep. (In Europe, the political elites of the European Union have been more responsive to the separationist vision, though demographic change makes the future of Europe increasingly cloudy.) How closely the opening up of the public square was tied to particular political factors—especially the political success of Republicans more open to a role for religion in the public square and the impact of Republican appointments to the Supreme Court—remains to be seen. Perhaps it is inevitable that with changing political fortunes of public figures who take varying stances on such issues, there will regularly be a need for other books like *The Naked Public Square.*

Part One

Religion and Politics:
The Contemporary Scene

1

The Public Square: Naked No More?

Gerard V. Bradley

Introduction

The year 1984 was the high-water mark of the Supreme Court's campaign to privatize religion, to construct what Richard John Neuhaus famously called "the naked public square." It was also the year that Neuhaus published the book of that name. Then the privatization tide began to roll out. *The Naked Public Square* contributed greatly to this welcome development, more than any other publication did. The book's broad learning, elegant expression, and ecumenical appeal established it immediately as a touchstone of debate and as a rallying point for those resisting the Court's secularizing initiative. The movement has since scored many victories. Neuhaus is justly celebrated as one of its leading impresarios.[1]

There is more to the ebbtide than the influence of publications, of course. The Court's first step in its privatization campaign was a political miscalculation.[2] That step was the 1962 ruling against school prayer. New York's public school students daily recited, "Almighty God we acknowledge our dependence upon thee, and we beg Thy blessings upon us, our parents, our teachers, and our Country." In *Engel v. Vitale*[3] the Supreme Court assumed no coercion of students was involved in these daily exercises. The Court did not hold that the prayer favored a particular religion. Even so, the Court held the prayer to be an unconstitutional "establishment of religion."

Engel christened a new master norm of church-state constitutional law: neither the states nor the federal government may promote or foster or aid religion, even if there is no coercion or preference among believers. This was "separation of church and state," and it meant mutual abstention of the two spheres. The state and its sphere were to be wholly secular; religious life was entirely private. Religion and politics were to operate along parallel arcs of mutually exclusive concerns.

Engel was a political mistake because it touched the third rail of American politics—evangelical Christians—awakening them from their long apolitical slumber. The Court's decision the next term against Bible reading (the *Schempp* case[4]) made the stakes more clear: the Court, it seemed, was bent on full-throated secularism. It took a decade for the political backlash to mature. But what we now call "the Christian right" was born in the school-prayer crucible.

The *Engel* Court was working against a perennial tradition of public religion in America, too. Since the Mayflower landed at Plymouth Rock, Americans have understood themselves, their experiment in liberty, and their country's role on the world historical stage in religious terms. America's public discourse up to and through the 1960s was tinged with religious rhetoric, imagery, and religiously sanctioned moral norms. The civil rights movement is perhaps the prime example. Even now, arguments about abortion, environmentalism, foreign policy, immigration reform, and welfare politics are all honeycombed with religious, and often strictly biblical, references, norms, and themes.

It could hardly be otherwise. Americans have very largely professed belief in the Bible as Scripture, as the Word of God. Even those who have professed other faiths or who were religiously indifferent still lived in a culture heavily indebted to the Bible—the Decalogue in particular—for moral norms. Biblical morality extends to questions of human rights, warfare, and caring for the needy and weak; it makes inescapable demands upon those exercising public authority. Even the Supreme Court conceded in the *Schempp* case that the "fact that the Founding Fathers believed devotedly that there was a God and [that] the unalienable rights of man were rooted in Him is clearly evidenced in their writings, from the Mayflower Compact to the Constitution itself."[5]

In light of these traditions, the American people and most of their political leaders judged the Court's privatizing initiative to be alien and just plain wrong. Americans had always, of course, understood religion to have indispensable private components; faith was at its core a voluntary, individual decision and experience, for example. But the notions that religion was wholly private and that public endorsement of it was unlawful never commanded wide adherence. The Court launched the campaign, however, with support from secularized elites in the legal academy, on the bench, and at the bar. By the mid-1980s, the Court had forfeited much of that support. One reason is that the corpus was a swollen mess. The rhetoric in it was increasingly strident, even hysterical. One opinion after another warned gravely that, but for the Court's "wall of separation," sanguinary religio-political conflict would incinerate us. It never did. In one case after another, the Court said that it dutifully implemented the unequivocal "command" of the Founders. Few in the academy believed it. Many did not care.

Then there were the case results, the dos and don'ts of church-state constitutional law. The accumulated holdings by 1990 threatened to collapse under the weight of their own incoherence. Church-state was the realm of legendary inconsistencies. The Court upheld bus rides for parochial school children to and from school but invalidated buses for field trips. Textbooks could be loaned to students in these schools, but maps could not be. (Yes, pundits raised the atlas question: what about a book *of* maps?) "Direct" aid to parochial schools was forbidden. "Indirect" aid was permitted. The principled difference between them was invisible to the eye.

By the time Justice Clarence Thomas wrote in 1995 that Establishment Clause jurisprudence was in "hopeless disarray,"[6] he echoed a chorus of critics from the bench, the bar, and the academy. In 2004 he amended his judgment: "Our jurisprudential confusion has led to results that can only be described as silly."[7] Thomas cited the example of *Allegheny v. American Civil Liberties Union*,[8] in which "the Court distinguished between a crèche on the one hand and an 18-foot Chanukah menorah near a 45-foot Christmas tree on the other. The Court held that the first display violated the Establishment Clause but that the second did not."[9]

I

The Supreme Court generated an audience for *The Naked Public Square* in 1984 by creating one. Four improbable and unpopular decisions during the 1984–85 term form the zenith of privatization. Each was extreme in outcome, strained in reasoning, and exaggerated in rhetoric.

The Court in *Caldor v. Thornton*[10] struck down a Connecticut statute which codified the Court's own free exercise holdings. Starting in 1963 in *Sherbert v. Verner*,[11] the Court had held that religious objections to employment duties, or an employee's religiously motivated refusal to labor on his or her Sabbath, could not count as the kind of "misconduct" for which discharge without unemployment compensation was the penalty. *Sherbert* initiated a line of decisions constituting what came to be known as the "conduct exemption" doctrine. This doctrine prescribed that nonconformity with any law because of religious scruples—even with laws having nothing to do with religion, such as those about unemployment compensation—was justified by the Free Exercise

Clause, *unless* the governing authority could prove to a judge that conformity was necessary to preserve a compelling state interest.

The Connecticut law in *Caldor* said that anyone who stated that a particular day of the week was his Sabbath could not be made to work on that day. Conscientious refusal to work on one's Sabbath could not lawfully be grounds for dismissal. All Sabbath observers were treated equally. All Sabbatarians were protected as the Court, seemingly, had sought to protect them, starting with *Sherbert v. Verner.* The Court in *Caldor* did not repudiate or modify the "conduct exemption" doctrine. (That doctrine was abandoned later, in the 1990 *Oregon v. Smith* decision.[12]) The Court nonetheless declared the Connecticut law unconstitutional, saying that it "impermissibly advances a particular religious practice"—"Sabbath observance."[13]

What was "impermissible" about it? One might speculate that the Court faulted Connecticut for favoring a "particular"—that is, *one*—"religious practice," for protecting *it* but not other religious practices. Perhaps the Court had in mind (without quite saying so) that the Connecticut law discriminated against religions having no Sabbath. In response, it could be said that one statute should not be expected to protect all religious practices. One burden upon religion is enough for one statutory remedy, the reply might hold. The *Caldor* Court made no effort anyway to survey other Connecticut statutes to see which additional religious practices were especially protected. The Court gave no hints about another "particular" religious observance which could have been advanced, but was not.

It turns out that the operative word in *Caldor* is "religious." The neglected party was not the non-Sabbatarian religious believer. The *Caldor* Court emphasized the peremptory quality of the exception: Sabbatarians had an "absolute" or "automatic" right to the day off; it was an "unyielding" preference. The central flaw in the law would remain, however, *even if* the preference were more pliable. The principle at stake concerned the *unbelieving* coworker: "other employees who have strong and legitimate, but nonreligious reasons for wanting a weekend day off have no rights under the statute."[14] Indeed they did not. Connecticut sought to promote the undisturbed exercise of *religion*; duck hunters and golfers were not on the agenda. In so doing Connecticut did what exemption statutes typically did, and what the Court in *Sherbert* indicated they should do: take care to protect religious believers from certain avoidable burdens. *Sherbert* exhibited no concern that nonreligious workers who lost jobs due to personal or health reasons receive protection comparable to—or even a fraction of—that accorded by the Court to believers. The Supreme Court nonetheless said in *Caldor* that workers seeking leisure or family time could not, consistent with the Constitution, be assigned a "back seat to the Sabbath observer."[15]

The Court apparently meant that it was unfair to employees who would have to cover the shifts (perhaps, when inconvenient) for excused Sabbatarians. This was, perhaps, little more than a supplementary argument. But it should nonetheless be asked: why is it unfair to provide concessions to believers that are not provided to nonbelievers? It is not unfair to give women maternity leave or national guardsmen a right to return to their jobs, so long as one holds that these activities (mothering, soldiering) are good, and that those performing them ought not to suffer on that account. The central premise of *Caldor* seems to be, then, that religion is simply one private activity among many others, all stipulated to possess the same value—or none—in the law's eyes.

The second of the four summit cases was *Wallace v. Jaffree*.[16] Some parents of children attending Mobile, Alabama, public schools challenged a statute authorizing a period of silent "meditation or voluntary prayer." The Court zeroed in on the fact that the phrase "or voluntary prayer" had been added to a statute pertaining (before amendment) to "meditation" only. The "effort to return voluntary prayer"—as the Court phrased it—to the schools would not do.

The reasoning of *Jaffree* is a puzzle. The Court's opinion maintained all of the following propositions: 1) not only is "voluntary prayer" in public schools constitutionally permissible, but also students have (according to the *Jaffree* Court) a "right to engage in voluntary prayer during an appropriate moment of silence during the schoolday";[17] 2) the state may constitutionally designate a moment of "silent meditation" during which students may pray; 3) the state may also (apparently) designate and/or announce to students that they may pray during the pause; and 4) Alabama violated the constitutional requirement of "neutrality" toward religion by *amending* an existing statute authorizing a period of silence for "meditation." The Court even observed (in a footnote) that "for some persons meditation itself may be a form of prayer."[18]

According to the Court, Alabama's lawmakers could have included "voluntary prayer" in the original legislative package without "endorsing" (the Court's evaluative term) religion. In the event, legislators added it later. But doing *that*, the *Jaffree* Court said, "endorsed" religion and therefore violated the Constitution. Adding it later also lacked a "secular" purpose.

The *Jaffree* Court made much of the evidence—and there was plenty—that the statutory amendment to make explicit the students' right to pray silently lacked a "secular" purpose. But why should that be so? Articulating the existence and/or scope of anyone's free exercise rights under the Constitution would seem to be a *legitimate* purpose. It would surely seem to be a constitutionally valid purpose. Whether it should or could also be called "secular" or "religious" is really beside the point.

Aguilar v. Felton[19] and *Grand Rapids School District v. Ball*[20] involved public assistance to parochial schools. In each case, local public authorities administered federal programs and funds for remedial and special education. In each case, public personnel entered parochial schools to teach kids who went there. The New York City teachers (in *Aguilar)* were dispatched to fulfill the school district's responsibility (under Title I of the landmark 1965 Johnson education act) to meet the "special needs" of *all* kids within the district. It did not matter under Title I where, or even if, needy kids attended school. If they resided within the geographical boundary of the public school district—and even if they were homeschooled—they had a right to services. Local public authority had a corresponding duty to provide the services.

The Supreme Court concluded that the Grand Rapids, Michigan, program "impermissibly advanced religion," chiefly because the public school personnel might "inculcate" the religion of the host school. This arrangement, said the Court, lacked the *public* supervisory control of these *public* teachers, necessary to keep them on the secularized straight and narrow. The case contained no information about the religious affiliation—if any—of the public teachers sent into the parochial schools. For all that the evidence showed, the worry would be that Jewish teachers (for example) would "inculcate" Catholicism when visiting, say, St. Rita's grade school. Nonetheless, this program "pose[d] a substantial risk of state-sponsored indoctrination" and of "symbolic union of church and state."[21]

New York's public educational officials met this concern head-on. They sent public supervisors into the schools to keep an eye on the teachers. Catch 22! Now the Supreme Court said that the supervision required to eliminate the risk of "inculcation"—the problem in *Grand Rapids*—was an impermissible entanglement! This "pervasive monitoring" allied the public school district too closely to the host parochial school, promoting what the Court called an "excessive entanglement" of church with state.

II

The improbable holdings of 1984–85 have been overruled or modified. The overheated rhetoric in them has cooled. Sober exchanges between justices about the Founding and religion have more recently emerged. One of the Court's major policy judgments pushing the privatizing cases was that *any* risk of promoting religion—however fantastic or hypothetical—was too great to bear. Its view was that faith is more volatile than nitroglycerine. This aversion to a whiff of incense near the public square has gone away. The Court is learning to live with God.

The whole conduct-exemption doctrine was overhauled in *Oregon v. Smith* (1990).[22] *Smith* abandoned *Sherbert* and progeny as interpretations of the Free Exercise Clause. For the *Smith* majority, this result was required by fidelity to the Founders' design. For once, the Court was right about the Founding (as I have argued at length elsewhere[23]).

Even so, the *Smith* opinion implied that *Caldor's* mandate to treat equally believers and bowlers was no longer the law; the *Smith* majority obviously anticipated that legislators would (as Connecticut's had in *Caldor*) exempt believers from some laws. Any doubt about the matter was eliminated by the unanimous decision in *Cutter v. Wilkinson* (2005),[24] which held (overruling the Sixth Circuit Court of Appeals) that the Religious Land Use and Institutionalized Persons Act of 2000—RLUIPA—was on its face a permissible accommodation of religion. In substance, RLUIPA protected both institutionalized persons (the plaintiff in *Cutter* was a prison inmate) and certain religious buildings from "substantial burdens" imposed by law. These burdens were unlawful unless they were justified by a "compelling governmental interest" and amounted to the "least restrictive means" of achieving such an interest. The Court affirmed in *Cutter* that free exercise did not require "conduct exemptions." (That is what *Smith* had held.) *Cutter* distinguished the holding in *Caldor*. The Court also said that the Sixth Circuit "misread our precedents" to prohibit "giving greater protection to religious rights than to other constitutionally protected rights."[25] The *Cutter* Court concluded that the Establishment Clause permitted accommodations to believers even where they do not "come packaged with benefits to secular entities."[26]

Agostini v. Felton[27] in 1997 expressly overruled *Aguilar v. Felton*. In *Agostini* the Court abandoned the worry that public school personnel would indoctrinate kids in the host school's faith. The spigots of public aid to religious schools are open, and they are more than trickling. Substantial assistance to the institutions is permitted, so long as it is not directed toward religious activity as such.[28] Vouchers and other forms of payments directly to parents are also permitted.[29] Cases starting in earnest with the 1993 *Lamb's Chapel*[30] decision eliminated almost all discrimination against *private* religious expression in public spaces. If the mall or the park or the statehouse lawn is made available to speakers on nonreligious topics, no discrimination against religious viewpoints on those topics is permitted. If a public library opens a meeting room to discussions of "family life," it may not exclude the likes of Dr. James Dobson due to his religious "viewpoint" on the subject.[31] All sorts of other benefits must be equally available to believers and religious groups so long as the class of beneficiaries is defined without reference to religion. If a public university chooses to fund student magazines, for example, *Rosenberger v. Rectors* held that it may not deny funds to magazines which offer a Christian viewpoint on current events.[32]

The Court's retreat from the 1984 summit is far from complete. There is still a lot of very important work to be done. Let us take stock. *Smith* belongs in a category by itself. The decision turned on the majority's commitment to a certain method of constitutional interpretation, basically to originalism—the view that courts today should seek the basic principles and norms of constitutional adjudication in the settled public understanding of the relevant constitutional terms when they were enacted. The historical evidence persuaded these justices that the Founders said "no" to judicially mandated conduct exemptions. And there was an end to it. We should believe that, if the evidence had been different, these same justices would have ruled differently. There is also lively disagreement about whether the "conduct exemption" itself indicates devotion to the privatizing campaign or not.[33] That the very strict-separationist Justice John Paul Stevens provided the fifth vote in *Smith* is important to remember. For these reasons, *Smith* offers only circumstantial evidence of anti-privatizing tendencies of the Court.[34]

The other improvements just noted—*Lamb's Chapel, Rosenberger, Agostini*—all have to do with *private* religion's welcome in the public square, *between* church and state, *between* the religious individual and religious viewpoints, on one hand, and public resources on the other. The government may not discriminate against believers who are eligible for some public benefit or privilege available under a *nonreligious* description (such as "private school" or "applicant for parade permit" or "extracurricular club"). The government may assist (within limits) private-sector educators who satisfy compulsory school attendance laws, even if the recipient is a religious institution. When all is said and done, it is still the constitutional law that public authority may not aid or promote religion precisely *as such* (though *Cutter* does establish that legal burdens on the religious may be removed without a corresponding benefit to the nonreligious). In that important sense, it is still a naked public square. In fact, the real test of the public square's continuing nakedness remains to be taken. The litmus question is whether the government itself may affirm (say, acknowledge, recognize) in its own voice that there *is* a greater than human source of meaning and value—God.

Several frequently litigated issues raise this question. These include public school graduation prayers, municipal nativity scenes, legislative prayer, the Decalogue displayed on public grounds, and the phrase "under God" in the Pledge of Allegiance. None necessarily forces the issue because courts are adept at insulating any positive constitutional evaluation or express allowance or permission of such matters from a straight "thumbs up" to the litmus question. Courts say that the Decalogue, for instance, has played an important role in the development of our law. It is that role—and not anything about true divine provenance—that is recollected by public display of the two tables. Courts say that legislative prayer "solemnizes" an occasion; its function is to concentrate lawmakers' minds. The prayer's truth and even its status as a precisely *religious* exercise are irrelevant. Courts say—at least, some on the Supreme Court did in a 2004 case—that "under God" is a rhetorical decoration which links us to our past, a time gone by when people *did* affirm God and His Providence. In this view, the pledge's contemporary meaning is far from both its past as well as its literal sense.[35]

The *Engel* Court launched the privatization project by creating the litmus test. The privatizing plaintiffs' lawyer came before the Court professing devotion to religious liberty. The only way to do that, William Butler said during his oral argument, was to "keep religion out of our public life."[36] Later in the argument, Butler was asked by an unidentified justice: "Is it your position that our public schools, by virtue of our Constitution, are frankly secular institutions?" Butler's answer: "Absolutely yes." That is, Butler said, my "ultimate position."[37]

The prayer's defenders made the contrast as clear as it could be made. Bertram Daiker represented school officials, and he said, "[H]ere is where my friend [Butler] and I depart in our thinking. Since the earliest days of this country, going back to the Mayflower Compact, the men who put our country together have publicly and repeatedly recognized the existence of a Supreme Being, a God."[38] Later Porter Chandler stood up for some parents intervening to support the prayer. He said that petitioners "are now seeking . . . to eliminate all reference to God from the whole fabric of our public life and of our public educational system."[39] Their strategy was, like Butler's, to present the Court with a momentous choice about secularism. The difference was that these lawyers thought the naked public square too much for the Court to bear.

They were wrong. All of the justices, except for Potter Stewart, seemed to be on Butler's side. Stewart saw that it was a winner-take-all case. He pressed Butler hard to distinguish the Regents prayer at issue in *Engel* from the phrase "I pledge allegiance to . . . one nation under God." Butler faltered. He faltered too when Stewart pressed him to distinguish other divine adornments of public life—"in God We Trust," "God Save This Honorable Court," and the like.[40] Stewart and Butler thus served up to the Court the litmus test: may public authority assert that there is a God and that this God guides us?

Justice Hugo Black wrote the Court's opinion, and he eschewed two limited grounds for validating the prayer. "[N]either the fact that the prayer may be denominationally neutral nor the fact that its observance on the part of the students is voluntary can serve to free it from the limitations of the Establishment Clause, as it might from the Free Exercise Clause."[41] The point of the Establishment Clause, Black wrote, was to forestall "union" of government and religion, and thus to leave "religious functions to the people themselves and to those the people choose to look for religious guidance."[42] The Establishment Clause expresses the "principle" that religion is "too personal, too sacred, too holy, to permit its unhallowed perversion by a civil magistrate."[43] Except that "unhallowed perversion" was not a sorting tool. The Court's ruling made clear that *whenever* the civil magistrate gets involved with religion, it *is* an "unhallowed perversion." The *Engel* Court erected "the naked public square."

Justice Stewart alone dissented. He could not see "how an 'official religion' is established by letting those who want to say a prayer say it."[44] He had pressed Butler hard about the pledge and now wove the question into his opinion. The national motto, the "Star-Spangled Banner," and "under God" were all at stake, he said. And the validity of them all was "summed up by this Court just ten years ago in a single sentence: 'We are a religious people whose institutions presuppose a Supreme Being,'"[45] quoting from the Court's 1952 *Zorach v. Clausen* decision.[46]

III

The Supreme Court in *Elk Grove Unified School District v. New-dow*[47] avoided deciding the question of whether a California public school's practice of having children recite the Pledge of Allegiance was unconstitutional. The specific question was whether the phrase "under God," which Congress added to the pledge in 1954, violated the Establishment Clause. The Court did not answer it. Five justices voted to dismiss the case on procedural grounds. These justices decided that the plaintiff did not have standing to sue on his daughter's behalf because he did not have custody of her. (His ex-wife did.) The result in *Newdow* defers the constitutional question until the arrival of a proper plaintiff. One should not be hard to find. "Under God" is destined to come back to court. *Engel* and the naked public square will then be in the dock. What is likely to happen?

No one on the present Court is likely to join Justice Thomas in "rethinking the Establishment Clause" along federalism lines. Thomas observed in *Newdow* that "the Establishment Clause is best understood as a federalism provision": it "protects state establishments from federal interference but does not protect any individual right."[48] There is considerable historical evidence in favor of this view; scholars as able as Princeton's Robert George have argued the case.[49] No one on the Court, however, concurred in this part of Thomas's opinion.[50] It is unlikely that either of the appointees since *Newdow*—Chief Justice Jim Roberts and Justice Samuel Alito—will join Thomas, either. In some important sense they are both "conservatives," as is Thomas. It is a safe bet that both are fed up with Establishment Clause jurisprudence. (Everybody is.) And perhaps one or both of them is sympathetic to the history which Thomas treated as pivotal. But neither Roberts nor Alito is so strongly committed to the originalism that drove Thomas's analysis. They would have to be to go along with Thomas. It is scarcely conceivable that either would adopt a conclusion so far out of the mainstream, and which would require them to repudiate so much settled law, save on overriding methodological grounds.

The most important question about the "federalism" reading is, in my judgment, its meaning. A summary account of that reading might be "Congress has no power over religion in the states." But what does that mean? Does the "federalism" reading imply that Congress is under no Establishment Clause constraint when legislating *outside* of the states? Could Congress have established the Anglican Church in, say, the Oklahoma territory in 1900? Or in Washington, D.C., today? Could Congress now deny federal income tax deductions for contributions to Islamic mosques? Is the norm of sect equality (which many have argued is the correct reading of the establishment clause[51]) entirely out of the picture? Neither Justice Thomas nor anyone else on the *Newdow* Court considered this possible implication of the "federalism" reading of the Establishment Clause.

Chief Justice William Rehnquist voted to resolve *Newdow* on the merits. He would have upheld "under God." But Rehnquist did not reject the naked public square. He did not defend it. He tacked around the litmus question by denying that recitation of "under God" was necessarily a religious affirmation.

Rehnquist recognized that many people when they say the pledge, mean that "God has guided the destiny of the United States," or that the "United States exists under God's authority."[52] Rehnquist also catalogued evidence of Americans' perennial belief in God's providential care for our nation. But these meanings were not authoritative. Rehnquist wrote that the phrase "under God" does not convert the pledge into a "religious exercise."[53] The pledge is in "no sense a prayer, nor an endorsement of any religion." It is a "patriotic exercise": "a declaration of belief in allegiance and loyalty to the United States flag and [to] the Republic that it represents."[54] Of the historical evidence, the chief justice said that "all of these events strongly suggest that our national culture allows public recognition of our Nation's religious history and character."[55] The chief justice selected one of the few passages from the House proceedings on the bill to add "under God" to the Pledge that trafficked in the same kind of third-person report about what *others* were up to: "From the time of our earliest history our peoples and our institutions have reflected the traditional concept that our Nation was founded on a fundamental belief in God."[56]

Several layers of hearsay insulate the Chief Justice's analysis. "Our institutions," a "traditional concept," our "national culture" and more stand between Rehnquist's approving vote and a living affirmation that God exists.

Justice Sandra Day O'Connor considered the merits of the *Newdow* lawsuit too. Whether it was on the basis of intuition or judgment (or both), she clearly wanted to uphold the pledge intact. She wanted also to retain *Engel*'s "neutrality" between religion and nonreligion—the naked public square. Where Chief Justice Rehnquist evinced little interest in the litmus question, O'Connor was keen to affirm the answer on offer since *Engel*: no favorable government recognition of religion is permissible because the state must be scrupulously neutral between belief and unbelief. O'Connor struggled to find a spot in the naked public square for "under God." Given her commitment to *Engel*, she needed a shoehorn. Her contorted opinion shows its effects.

At some points in *Newdow*, O'Connor seemed to mimic Rehnquist's avoidance technique of reporting that, for some other people, "under God" was or is a living affirmation. She said that "[e]ven if taken literally, the phrase is merely descriptive; it purports only to identify the United States as a Nation subject to divine authority."[57] This seemed to O'Connor to be a permissible "religious acknowledgment." It was not a "prayer," which O'Connor defined as "a solemn avowal of divine faith and supplication for the blessings of the Almighty." "Under God" was not a "serious invocation of God," either. It did not put the "speaker or listener in a penitent state of mind." It was not intended to "create a spiritual communion or invoke divine aid."[58]

O'Connor's path in *Newdow* was nonetheless unique. Her main point was that "under God" belongs to the class of expressions called "ceremonial deism": "references [which] speak the language of religious belief, [but which] are more properly understood as employing the idiom for essentially secular purposes."[59] By "ceremonial deism" O'Connor did *not* seem to mean that "under God" actually is, despite surface appearances, really a wholly secular expression. Someone who says "Good God!" at the ballpark communicates surprise or awe at a monstrous home run; he or she is not asserting anything about divine attributes. The exclamation "Holy cannoli" has nothing to do with the sacred or with pastry for that matter. It is an expression with a pretty clear meaning: "Wow!" In these cases the real meaning of the phrase is not the literal one.

Our language and culture are suffused with religious allusions and symbols that have lost their religious denotations. They now have stable secular meanings. These include many biblical references, such as the symbol of the American Medical Association (the caduceus, from the Book of Numbers); the phrase "handwriting on the wall" (from the Book of Daniel); and the phrase "apple of my eye" (one of God's Old Testament descriptions of his chosen people, Israel). No one now says that the government endorses Judaism when these phrases are used, because of their origins in the Old Testament.

The names of many cities in the United States (Los Angeles, San Francisco) literally call to mind holy beings. Their origins lie in Roman Catholic practice and belief. But no one seriously thinks that these names violate the Establishment Clause. Once in a while a constitutional challenge is mounted against some such city. But lawsuits of the sort are dismissed in court and branded as absurd reductios by observers outside.

The problem for Justice O'Connor was that she was stuck with a phrase which has *not* passed into the safe harbor of secular idiom. "Under God" is not like San Antonio. "Under God" is still "facially religious." Her key strategic move was to say that "facially religious references can serve . . . valuable purposes in public life."[60] These purposes are secular. O'Connor identified two for "under God." One secular purpose is to "commemorate the role of religion in our history."[61] The other is to "solemn[ize] public occasions." She said that "[f]or centuries, we have marked important occasions or pronouncements with references to God and invocations of divine assistance."[62] Oddly, O'Connor then said that these references serve "[to] solemnize an occasion instead of to invoke divine providence."[63] Most charitably read, O'Connor was here saying that "solemnity"—a secular end—can be obtained by invoking God. As she said a little later in her opinion, "The constitutional value of ceremonial deism turns on a shared understanding of its legitimate nonreligious purposes."[64]

Religious means to secular ends. The mainstream of Establishment Clause jurisprudence before *Newdow* held that "endorsing" religion—even where doing so had some useful consequences—was unconstitutional. No one in the *Grand Rapids* or *Aguilar* majorities, for example, denied that special education for parochial school children was good or that special education was a valid secular purpose. But the Court held there that the state was not constitutionally permitted to achieve a good end by the bad means of "symbolically" uniting church and state. Indeed, if "endorsing" religion is permissible so long as it is useful, then the aid to religious schools would, as a general matter, be fine: no one has ever doubted that these schools provide sound secular instruction along with religious training. The burden of O'Connor's *Newdow* opinion, then, would be the need to place principled limits on the possibility of using religious means to secular ends. The category "ceremonial deism" cannot really help her. It is a conclusion, not a test or a standard. It is what you call it when you want to make an exception to the prevailing occupancy rules in the naked public square. And she cut off aid from another plausible source when she said (even emphasized) that there "are no *de minimis* violations of the Constitution—no constitutional harms so slight that the courts are obliged to ignore them."[65]

Let's look a bit more closely now at the first purpose— "commemorat[ing] the role of religion in our history." Because of our history as a religious nation, Justice O'Connor said, "eradicating such references [as 'under God'] would sever ties to [our] history." Maybe so. It is certainly true that cultivating a certain idiom—form, style, and language of expression—might be necessary to gain effective access to the history of a family, church, or nation. One may have to study ancient languages to really understand the Bible. One must be familiar with ancient Jewish customs and Middle Eastern history to really understand the New Testament. Some understanding of Greek philosophical concepts is needed if one is to really understand parts of the Gospel of John.

Given the role of Christians and Christianity in our nation's history, that history may be obscure to anyone who is innocent of the Bible and of Christian theology. Even so, it would still be contrary to the Court's holdings to stage daily Bible recitation in public schools. Daily instruction in the history of Christianity would scarcely pass muster in court, too, even if it could be persuasively argued that students could not understand "religion's role in our history" without it. Why is the pledge different?

Besides, everyday recitation of the two words "under God" is *not* a bridge to our past. It is too curt and untutored for that. What does it really tell students that they do not already know but need to know? Perhaps with this in mind, O'Connor said in *Newdow* that "under God" "ties" us to a "history" which "sustains this Nation today."[66] She illustrated her point by reference to a passage from the *Allegheny* case, where the Court was concerned not to "sweep away all government recognition and acknowledgment of the role of religion in the lives of our citizens."[67] But the *Allegheny* Court meant the lives of *today's* citizens. *Allegheny* found room enough in the public square for a frank recognition of religion and its role in the lives of modern Americans. *Allegheny* was not about linking today's secularized (by hypothesis, at least) Americans with their more God-fearing ancestors, as O'Connor seems to suggest in *Newdow*. O'Connor may have flirted here with upholding the pledge as a living affirmation of some propositions about God, Providence, and America today—a flirtation contrary to Establishment Clause doctrine but a tolerable *de minimis* departure from good form. But she could not quite let herself consummate the deal. Her commitment to the naked public square stopped her.

Justice O'Connor sought in *Newdow* to reconcile the pledge with her "endorsement" test. Her "endorsement" test asks the following: does "the ceremony or representation . . . convey a message to a reasonable observer, familiar with its history, origins, and context, that those who do not adhere to its literal message are political outsiders,"[68] are not "full members of the political community,"[69] or are second-class citizens? It is not that O'Connor required every government religious expression to serve this purpose. It is more that "endorsement" constitutes a strict condition. The "endorsement" test is thus a test for or criterion of "civil religion"; at least it would limit all apparently religious expression by the government according to a political functional standard, sounding in equality.

How does this procedure serve O'Connor's stated goal to free America's believers from political pressure to conform? It could scarcely be the case that the Constitution requires, or even permits, the government somehow to effect a change in persons' religious beliefs, such that Jehovah's Witnesses or Amish Anabaptists (for example) come to view themselves as "political insiders." They do not want to be. They want to be outsiders, if not quite "second-class citizens." And the ostensible purpose of much of the Court's work for decades has been to let them be so.

Cornell historian R. Laurence Moore shows in his superb book *Religious Outsiders and the Making of Americans* that it is not just fringe sects which consciously seek "outsider" status. "Outsiderhood," Moore argues, "is a characteristic way of inventing one's Americanness."[70] He cites the tendency of Americans to express their "most cherished convictions in the language of dissent." "New religions," too, "have served as vehicles through which people have nurtured a sense of antagonistic culture."[71] Moore's arguments and evidence do not justify government discrimination against—or even stigmatization of—a class of believers. His work does suggest, however, the need to ask further critical questions about the "endorsement" test, especially to probe whether its aspiration to include is meant to serve Caesar more than it is to serve individual conscience.

IV

Justice Thomas was right on the mark when he said in *Newdow* that "it is difficult to see how [saying 'one nation under God'] does not entail an affirmation that God exists."[72] Thomas's view is the commonsense understanding of "under God," as Rehnquist explicitly recognizes and as O'Connor implicitly must have. The commonsense view is also the historically correct one. "Under God" was not added by Congress in 1954 to establish links to the past. "Under God" was not added to "commemorate the role of religion in our history." "Under God" was added to make a statement about Americans' present unity and distinct national identity. The pledge was not amended in 1954 mainly to reflect what was *ours*. That was part of it. But "under God" was added primarily because, and on the strict understanding that, it was *true*. "Under God" meant that we were indeed "one nation under God."

The pledge amendment was the first of three 1950s episodes in which Congress sought to identify, affirm, and reinforce the ground *outside* of law, government, and the Constitution *for* them. Congress sought in these episodes sources, presuppositions, implications, entailments, ulterior convictions. Nothing important depends upon selecting any one of these characterizations. The important thing is that the quest was not satisfied in or by tradition, consensus, or principles animating the Constitution or even the Founding. To be sure, nothing derogatory about any of these venerable sources of inspiration was implied by the congressional activity. They received favorable mention on a regular basis. But tradition, consensus, and the Founding were not terminal points in the quest; quite the contrary, it was assumed to be the case that they all possessed a further meaning and value. The real terminal point was a *transcendent reality* upon which our whole political life—institutions, laws, practices, and ideals—finally depends.

The relationship between polity and transcendent source of meaning was both theoretical (pertaining to a coherent and full understanding or to what is needed to make sense of our polity) and practical (how things go in this world depends upon getting right with the Creator and Ruler of all that there is). "One nation under God" is a very compact expression for a set of ideas I call the "metaphysics of liberty."

The historical impetus for amending the pledge was the Cold War. Congressman Louis Rabaut of Michigan testified at a committee hearing: "Remember, when you hear your own children recite the pledge, these same words could not come from little Muscovite children standing before the red, hammer and sickle flag of Soviet Russia."[73] Congressman Walter B. Jones later in the same hearing made the matter more plain: Could the Communists "adopt the pledge of allegiance to the flag as it exists now? They could use that pledge of allegiance and apply it to the sickle and the hammer. But if you have 'under God' you would stymie them."[74] Rabaut again: "[T]he one fundamental issue which is the unbridgeable gap between America and Communist Russia is belief in Almighty God."[75]

This testimony may sound to us like an oversimplified morality tale, even bad theater. Up to a point it was. But to these historical actors, it was all a deadly serious business, a matter of succinctly establishing what we were fighting for. In those days of nuclear brinksmanship, it was also what we were risking everything for. There was nothing of McCarthyism in it, no expressed worries about reds under the bed or in the State Department. Nor was the "liberty" in this metaphysic reactionary or conservative. Religion was an essential piece of our national identity. But in these hearings there was no suggestion that everyone should actually be religious. The point was educative, not devotional. It was that Americans should know what America was all about.

Representative John Pillion of New York said that our

> western civilization is a product of the Christian-Judaic conception of the individuality and dignity of every human soul. The liberalism of our constitutional form of government, in turn, is the product and the beacon light of western civilization and its acceptance of one God with universal and supreme spiritual significance."[76]

The 1954 House Committee Report on the "under God" amendment confirmed Pillion's account:

> Our American Government is founded on the concept of the individuality and the dignity of the human being. Underlying this concept is the belief that the human person is important because he was created by God and endowed by him with certain inalienable rights which no civil authority may usurp. The inclusion of God in our pledge would further acknowledge the dependence of our people and our government upon the moral directions of the Creator.[77]

The pledge amendment was part of a mid-fifties triptych, each panel displaying the metaphysics of liberty from a remarkably similar angle. In 1955, Congress made a law out of the prevailing practice of inscribing all currency with "In God We Trust." One sponsor of the legislation—Florida's Charles Bennett—testified before the House Banking Committee about "these days when imperialistic and materialistic communism seeks to attack and destroy freedom."[78] Our response should be, Bennett said, to "continuously look for ways to strengthen the foundations of our freedom."[79]

Bennett found footings right where backers of the pledge amendment did: "At the base of our freedom is our faith in God and the desire of Americans to live by His will and by His guidance," Bennett concluded. The committee chair (Brent Spence) credited the guiding hand of God for "our Constitution . . . because in all history there was never a charter like ours, there never was one that served for so long the best interests of millions of people."[80]

In 1956, the other shoe hit the floor: "In God We Trust" was declared the national motto. Representative Bennett was again hard at work. He testified in 1956 that while laboring on the currency bill, he discovered that we had no national motto. "In God We Trust" had been recognized officially on various occasions but had never been adopted precisely as our motto. Its claim to recognition was bolstered, Bennett testified, by its position in the fourth stanza of the national anthem: "And this be our motto, in God is our trust." He repeated (verbatim) his 1955 "these days" speech. But this time he added that "more than any other phrase it expresses the spiritual and moral values upon which our country was founded and upon which it depends for survival."

Statements such as those in the preceding paragraphs concealed some degree of disagreement. Persons equally devoted to these sentiments could be categorized according to one's emphasis upon Communism's smothering of individuality (call this a "liberal" emphasis) or upon the Soviets' threat to the whole American way of life (call this a more "conservative" emphasis). Still, the consensus around the proposition that our Cold War adversaries—chiefly the Soviet Union—meant to erase God from human consciousness straddled ordinary political divisions.

Do these Cold War episodes amount to a "civil religion"? Let us stipulate that by "civil religion" we mean, centrally, the capture (subordination, compromise) of God and his transcendent will by the imperatives of the polity. I think the answer to the question about the fifties is, then, yes and no.

Yes. The fifties' episodes involve a close identification between the transcendent source of meaning and value and American society. No one in any of the three episodes expressed doubt about which side God was on. The absence of this blithe connection is one striking thing about Lincoln's Second Inaugural Address, the archetypical public expression which is *not* a "civil religion." Our congressmen did not submit, as did Lincoln, to an unpredictable if not inscrutable Providence. "Both [sides in the Civil War] read the same Bible and pray to the same God," said Lincoln. And each invokes His aid against the other." Though it may seem strange that men who hold other men in bondage should ask divine assistance, "let us judge not, that we may not be judged. The Almighty has His own purposes."

Words such as these could never have passed the lips of Congressman Rabaut and friends. After all, the Soviets did not read the Bible.

No. Neither Lincoln nor our congressmen made superficial appeals to transient gods of political fortune. Perhaps there are no atheists in foxholes. Perhaps in wars hot and cold there are few public figures willing to dissent openly from the earnest expression of pieties. Even so, the appeals of the mid-fifties were sincere and, by every indication, representative of the American public's sentiments. They were not a tactic or strategy in the Cold War. They were not pieces of propaganda at a rally. It was not "praise the Lord and pass the ammunition." They were instead succinct analyses of what the unprecedented threat of Armageddon was *about.* In other words, the metaphysics of liberty were recited because they were thought to be true, not because they were ours.[81] It is especially important to note, too, that these truths did not depend for their accessibility or for their validity upon revelation or religious authority. (That is partly why they were considered nonsectarian.) In fact, they were considered to be available to unaided reason—"natural" religion.

V

Is it unconstitutional for public authority to affirm basic religious truths available to reason? Does public authority violate the

Establishment Clause by asserting such propositions as that God exists and that God has a benevolent plan for humankind?

It is misguided to say that the national Constitution requires government affirmation of basic religious truths. There is no such command in the language of the Constitution. None is implied. This apparent constitutional abstention on matters of faith does not reflect, however, a Founding which was, somehow, incipiently or inchoately committed to "privatizing" religion. Not at all. The Constitution's apparent secularism owes principally to what Justice Thomas suggested in *Newdow*: public authority to care for religion belongs mainly to the *states*.

A glance at state constitutions shows more than an expectation that the government would affirm certain basic religious truths. Those constitutions—now and then—*contain* such affirmations. The state constitutional settlements included the political community's affirmation of certain *natural* truths about God. The divine realities affirmed in the Declaration of Independence—a unitary God who created all there is, who providentially guides human events, and whose effects include naturally known moral truths—could be and were known by reason alone. These truths are elements of a "natural theology" or "natural religion"—really a branch of philosophy. Promoting respect for and belief in them was part of the common good entrusted to the care of public authority. A glance at what Congress and presidents have done since 1789 robustly shows that, where the national government had authority to care for religion—in territories, in the District of Columbia, in military and foreign affairs—such affirmations were commonplace.[82]

As the 1950s episodes confirm, our institutions call for and depend upon the metaphysics of liberty. Saying so has seemed, in season and out, to be appropriate, fitting, and right.

The political community's common life did not extend, however, to matters which distinguished the various churches from one another. The Founders' most important insight into religious liberty as a civil right was to see that the truth about sectarian matters—sacred doctrine, modes of worship, forms of church polity, rules for church membership in good standing—did not pertain to the common good. These matters could safely be kept out of political life. They were not unimportant. Arbitrating them need not be, however, the civil magistrate's task. Theologians might contend over the details of faith and worship. But the statesman could treat them as matters of opinion.

The most succinct Supreme Court statement of the Founders' constitutional doctrine on religion is from *Watson v. Jones*, an 1871 church property decision in which the Court declared that the general principle of constitutional law on religious liberty was that "the law knows no heresy, and is committed to the support of no sect, no dogma."[83] The Founders engineered their constitutional plan for church and state around the word and reality of *sect*. Views on such distinctly religious matters as the content of creeds and books of doctrine, liturgy or modes of worship, styles of church governance (hierarchical or congregational, national or local or regional), and internal church discipline (what qualifies or disqualifies an adherent for community membership) were all—in the law's eyes—to be treated as neither true nor false. Doctrine, discipline, worship, and governance were within the province of faith, characteristic of the sects. Contending accounts of these subjects were matters of opinion. Heresy and dogma were theological concepts. They were not legally cognizable. The doctrines of (say) Presbyterians, Catholics, and Jews were neither "dogma" nor "heresy," even if adherents of those faiths said so (of the others), and even if (because some of the doctrines were incompatible) one or more of them actually had to be false.

The Founders took the possibility of religious truth seriously. They put sectarian matters outside of the competence of the government, but they did not thereby denigrate them. They stipulated a sort of mental discipline for lawmakers. The First Amendment obliged those exercising public authority to refrain from making the truth or falsity of theological propositions a basis for legislation. This could be difficult for members of the

Founding generation. By and large they held that such matters were propositions: assertions which could be either true or false. The First Amendment meant that the truth (or falsity) of such matters had to be put aside in civil affairs; it neither stipulated nor supposed that the truth (or falsity) of these things did not exist. The amendment said that the validity of these propositions (though not of natural theological truths) was beyond the competence of public authority.

The Founders' decision to promote a full-dress public square is all the more extraordinary because of what they thought about religion. American religion has not been (until recently, perhaps) an aggregate of private spiritualities, just so many ineffable experiences of the "inner light." American religion was instead a highly cognitive enterprise, lodged within organizations with long histories, dynamic and strong internal imperatives (mined from sacred books, creeds, and theological traditions), and audible institutional voices. Some of these corporate bodies—Roman Catholicism and Anglicanism especially—had foreign sources of spiritual authority. Many more had large numbers of foreign adherents with whom the American body was in some sort of communion.

America's dominant religion—Christianity—has always taught that within the one political community there are two legitimate moral authorities, church and state. Indeed, as we briefly saw at the beginning of this essay, American religion has long been irreducibly *public* and inescapably intertwined with the rectitude of what the government says and does. The American states' collaboration with these free churches has been an often unquiet coexistence between independent forces, each with the resources to take care of itself and to contend with the other free of intimidation or undue deference. There has for these reasons never been any real possibility of an American Erastianism—state supremacy over religion such as there was in England, for example. Perhaps it is better to say that the only Erastianism *possible* in America would be the privatization of faith.

Justice O'Connor's *Newdow* opinion captured, more or less unwittingly, much of what the Founders wrought. She did not expressly trace her reflections to the Founding. But she echoed the Founders all the same. In fact, all her contortions to save the pledge while conserving *Engel* left her just one small analytical step from the Founders' settlement. The rhetorical gap was considerably wider, though it was still not a chasm.

O'Connor distinguished between what I have called "natural religion" and "sect." "Sectarian" comprises, O'Connor said, the "details upon which men and women who believe in a benevolent, omnipresent Creator and Ruler of the world are known to differ."[84] The pledge is not sectarian. It is "a simple reference to a generic God."[85] It does not refer to a "nation under Jesus" or "under Vishnu."[86] O'Connor upheld the "generic" reference, while stipulating that the affairs of sects were not government business. O'Connor could have used the term "natural religion" instead of "generic God." The substance of what she asserted would have been the same. And the substance of her "natural religion" was really quite robust; it even included an objective moral law—at least supposing that her "Ruler" promulgated some rules.

O'Connor could also have adopted Thomas's entailment: when school kids say "under God" they are talking about what they believe today (insofar as their recitation is not just rote). She could have upheld the pledge so understood without affirming that it is true. All that she would have to say to uphold the pledge is that those who amended the pledge in 1954, and those who called for schoolchildren to say it more recently, did so because *they* believed it to be true. There is a plausible basis for their belief, O'Connor would continue, and acting on it does not offend the Constitution.

O'Connor went almost this whole distance. The brake was her allegiance to the "endorsement" concept. Even here, though, she equivocated. O'Connor recognized that it was impossible to identify any "brief solemnizing reference" that "encompass[es] every religious belief expressed by any citizen of this Nation" (e.g., polytheism).[87] Universal inclusion was empirically unavailable. To uphold the pledge, O'Connor could have then turned to the Founders. For them, there was an objective common good in religion. There were common benefits to promoting belief in natural religion: religion was necessary to citizens' moral virtue, and without citizens' moral virtue, republican government was bound to fail. Whether some citizens felt left out or like second-class citizens was not especially pertinent, for the Founders understood that everyone enjoyed the fruits of a God-fearing citizenry. But to reason this way is to abandon the whole "endorsement" conundrum.

O'Connor would not take that step. She described "under God" as a "general acknowledgment of religion" which "reasonable observers" would not view as "denigrating the nonreligious." She could have and should have used "sectarian" as the principle limiting the scope of "ceremonial deism." She chose the non-endorsement standard instead.

Conclusion

The appeal of confused judicial reasoning lies, I suppose, in the appeal of the result obtained. O'Connor and Rehnquist (and Thomas, for that matter) reached the right result in *Newdow*. But this result could have been obtained through sound reasoning and without (as in the case of Justice Thomas) a quixotic attempt to steer Establishment Clause doctrine to where very, very few are likely to follow. The Founders' settlement and the traditions of the Court well into the twentieth century would have gotten the job done. The question is, then, whether unsound reasoning is the only way to obtain the right result.

The considerable benefits of a correct holding must be balanced against the harms of adding one more sediment of incoherence to the church-state morass. If nothing else, it is almost impossible to teach the area to law students without engendering in them deep cynicism about judicial decision-making. More generally, each unprincipled decision leads to a little more popular disrespect for the Court and for the law.

Here is one way of summarizing what O'Connor and Rehnquist did in *Newdow*: Upholding the pledge is very appealing. But sound reasoning in support of it collides with the naked public square. Abandoning the naked public square would be just too much for too many justices to bear. If put to a choice between the pledge and the naked public square, a majority of the Court would abandon the pledge, however unpopular that might be.

About this case the following question should be posed: would losing the pledge battle (because of a hypothesized insistence on sound reasoning, which would force the justices to reject either the pledge or the naked public square) really be a net loss in the war against the naked public square? Perhaps a result so obnoxious would lead more rapidly to real reform of the law (partly by reform of the Court under popular political pressure) than would another temporizing result.

2

The Naked Public Square Today: A Secular Public Square?

Mary Ann Glendon

In 1984's most popular action film, the hero travels back in time from the year 2024 in order to prevent a killer cyborg from carrying out an attempt to alter history. If the Terminator had not been foiled, Americans would have been headed for domination by semi-human creatures—conscienceless beings created by ourselves, but that by 2024 would escape human control.

While Richard John Neuhaus's 1984 book was concerned with more subtle threats to the American experiment, he too aimed at nothing less than shifting historical probabilities. His purpose was a double one: first, to warn that the growing tendency to rule religiously grounded moral viewpoints out of bounds in public life does injustice to what Neuhaus incorrigibly referred to as America's "incorrigibly religious" citizenry, and second, to draw attention to the danger that an overzealous secularization program poses to the cultural foundations of our republican form of government. Hence the subtitle of *The Naked Public Square*: *Religion and Democracy in America*.

Twenty-five years later, it is evident that Neuhaus and his associates have had an impressive influence on the debate about religion and public life. This symposium provides eloquent testimony to that fact. It is far less clear, however, that Neuhaus's ideas have been able to alter the legal and cultural developments about which he warned. As my contribution, I will offer some tentative thoughts, first, about whether the public square has become more or less open to the expression of religiously grounded moral viewpoints, and second, about whether we as a nation are doing better or worse at producing citizens and statespersons with the qualities that are required to sustain a republic with democratic elements. Those two questions intersect most dramatically in the field of education, and most of my remarks therefore will be addressed to issues in that field.

The Naked Public Square was, in good measure, a rallying cry. In 1984, it seemed to Neuhaus that the moment had come for men and women of faith to make themselves heard in setting the conditions under which free people order their lives together. He was heartened by what he saw as the growing political effectiveness of groups that were beginning to do just that. And he did his own part to encourage that trend by launching the interfaith ventures that became the Institute for Religion and Public Life and *First Things* magazine. At the time, such enterprises were rare. Today there are more than 150 organizations whose concerns fall under the heading of religion and public life.

Neuhaus's call to action was accompanied by a reminder that "[t]hose who wish to bring religiously based values to bear in public discourse have an obligation to 'translate' those values into terms that are as accessible as possible to those who do not share the same religious grounding."[1] If religious voices in the United States today are stronger, more confident, and more adept at translating their values into terms that are persuasive to their fellow citizens, more than a little credit must go to the encouragement and example of Neuhaus himself.

But it is not enough to have citizens who are willing and able to be in conversation with each other about the conditions under which we are to live, work, and raise our children. There must also be settings where such exchanges can regularly take place. How open is the public square today for conversation, contention, and compromise among a wide variety of moral actors?

The picture is mixed.

The religion decisions of the United States Supreme Court are so lacking in coherence that they are like tea leaves in which a reader can find some support for either his dearest hopes or his worst fears. Despite some evidence to the contrary, however, my own view is that since 1984, the Court has generally continued a six-decade-long trend toward confining religion to the private sphere.[2] By 1984, a number of legal scholars had exposed glaring defects in the line of cases where the Supreme Court, beginning in the 1940s, had set the two religion provisions of the First Amendment in opposition to each other, thus undermining the common value both provisions were designed to serve: religious freedom.[3] The lawyers' largely historical analyses were given a boost by Neuhaus, who, in another publication, pointed out that the "two clause" approach also flies in the face of a simple grammatical analysis of the text.[4] The First Amendment's religion language ("Congress shall make no law respecting an establishment of religion, or prohibiting the free exercise thereof. . . .") does not contain any clauses at all. It is a declarative sentence with two participial phrases. The most natural reading of the sentence, Neuhaus argued, is that both phrases were meant to work together in complementary fashion. The establishment language bars Congress from abridging religious freedom in a specific way (by legislation "respecting an establishment"), while the free exercise language bars Congress from limiting religious freedom in general.

Such arguments, however, have made little impression on a Supreme Court which continues to set the establishment and free exercise provisions at odds with each other—interpreting the establishment language broadly[5] and the free exercise guarantee narrowly[6]—to the detriment of both individual religious freedom and the freedom of religious groups to govern themselves. In 2004, the Court, in *Locke v. Davey*, actually gave its stamp of approval to official religious discrimination by permitting the state of Washington to single out the study of theology for exclusion from a public scholarship program.[7] Given the pervasive influence of governmental funding decisions in our society, the *Locke* decision has significant potential for a far-reaching, deleterious impact on religious freedom in general and voucher experiments in particular.[8]

It is not fanciful to imagine a Supreme Court majority following a course that could well end by reducing followers of many religions to something like *dhimmitude*—the status of non-Muslims in a number of Islamic countries. The *dhimmi* is tolerated so long as his religion is kept private and his public acts do not offend the state religion. Key positions in society are of course reserved for those who adhere to the official creed.

If we turn from the federal courts to developments within the elected branches of government, however, we find that some of Neuhaus's ideas have met a somewhat warmer reception. Certainly advocacy by Neuhaus and others on behalf of experiments with faith-based organizations has made considerable headway in recent years. In 1977, together with Peter Berger, he proposed a way around the impasse between proponents of a harsh laissez-faire approach to social services on the one hand and die-hard supporters of failing government programs on the other.[9] The hypothesis, which Berger and Neuhaus urged state and federal governments to test, was that health care, education, and other social services could be delivered more cheaply, effectively, and humanely through the mediating institutions of civil society, including religious institutions, than directly by the state.

That proposal, surely one of the most promising political ideas of the late twentieth century, found significant support within both the Clinton and Bush administrations. But efforts to put such experiments into practice with government funding have encountered formidable obstacles. On the one hand, religious institutions have been permitted to participate in many publicly funded programs of education, health care, housing, and services for the poor.[10] But the pressures on them to compromise their principles as the price of participation are often considerable.

The 2004 California Supreme Court decision requiring Catholic Charities of Sacramento to provide prescription contraceptive coverage in its employee health care plan is a case in point. The California court held that Catholic Charities was not religious enough to qualify for the statutory religious exemption.[11] Such issues seem likely to arise with increasing frequency with a real danger of requiring religious charities to choose between compromising their principles and abandoning their mission of service. Consider the New York City ordinance, enacted in 2004 over Mayor Michael Bloomberg's veto, which requires all organizations that contract with the city to provide benefits to unmarried domestic partners of employees.[12] Although the ordinance provides for an exception of sorts (if a religious organization provides benefits for "household members"), some providers of much-needed services have intimated that, rather than compromise their beliefs, they might cut back on their activities in New York. Equally troubling is the likelihood that some religious charities will devise ways to rationalize their acceptance of secular norms.

It is, I believe, in the field of *education* where one sees the most vivid illustrations of Neuhaus's point that a public square from which religion is banished will not long remain naked. The most important public square for most of this country's children is the elementary and secondary school system. And despite a few Supreme Court decisions on extracurricular activities,[13] it is hard to think of any public settings from which religion has been more rigorously excluded or where secularism is more dogmatically promulgated.[14] The legal and practical obstacles facing parents trying to exercise what the Supreme Court has recognized as their "fundamental interest . . . to guide the religious future and education of their children" are so great as to effectively deny that right to all but a few.[15]

When one considers that most children spend more waking hours in school than with their parents, and that many public schools actively proselytize against the most deeply held convictions of many religions, it is obvious why schools have become the chief battlegrounds for the struggle over the role of religion, not only in public life, but in private life as well. As Stephen Carter wrote in an essay for *First Things*, liberalism ceases to be liberal when it "not only dismisses [many Americans'] most cherished beliefs from the public sphere but even tries, through the device of public education, to make it harder for these beliefs to function in the private sphere."[16]

What are parents to do now that public schools and the media make it so difficult to transmit their culture to their own children? At present, the right to withdraw one's children from government-controlled education can be exercised only by parents determined and capable enough to undertake homeschooling or wealthy enough to afford private education after paying taxes to support government schools. That fact, together with the deficiencies of many public schools, has led to increased interest in a specific application of the Berger-Neuhaus proposal: voucher programs. It was an important advance for experiments with parental choice when the Supreme Court held in 2002 that the First Amendment's establishment provision was not violated by a voucher program that included religious schools.[17] But such programs are still few and far between. They have been vigorously opposed by teachers' unions, and they have been blocked in a majority of states by constitutional amendments, dating from the Know-Nothing era, that are interpreted to bar vouchers as aid to religion.[18]

No one should pretend that the issues in this area are easy to resolve. The way they are resolved, however, will have important implications for religious freedom, for parents' rights, and for the future of the democratic experiment.

So far as the public schools are concerned, the prevailing secularist approach does offer a solution to some real problems. In a pluralist society like ours, there are obviously limits to the degree to which public education can accommodate the religious diversity of the families it serves. The more heterogeneous our population becomes, moreover, the more need we have to shore up a sense of shared values and common purposes. The simplest way to deal with the first of those challenges is to keep all religion out of the public schools. That approach is often presented as "neutral" and respectful of pluralism. Whatever else may be said about official secularism, however, it is neither neutral nor hospitable to diversity.[19] As legal scholar Stephen Smith has pointed out, "Starting with an emphasis on pluralism, ironically, the theorists favoring [the secularist] positions in effect try to wish pluralism away."[20] What needs to be recognized is that secularism in the public schools involved the establishment of a new value system through a process of which parents had little notice and in which they had little voice. Whether intended or not, secularism in the public schools is a program for formation of persons, and thus a program for cultural transformation.

The great unanswered questions about all this are: What sort of person is the new system forming and what kind of society are we bringing into being? What are the implications for civic life of the transformation of this country's once vaguely Protestant public schools into secular government schools? Will those schools promote the traits a system of self-government requires in its citizens? Or will they merely socialize them in the ideology of a dominant class?

These questions are seldom asked, but they did engage the attention of John Stuart Mill in the most neglected section of his famous essay *On Liberty*. It is a pity that so few persons who pin their hopes for a free society on public education seem to have pondered the last section of Mill's essay, the chapter on "Applications," where he explained why he believed that it was essential, for the sake of liberty, to leave it up to parents to decide where and how their children will be educated. The danger that Mill feared was not *religion* in the schools but *government* in the schools. Here is what he wrote about the dangers of letting government get control over education:

All that has been said of the importance of individuality of character, and diversity in opinions and modes of conduct, involves, as of the same unspeakable importance, diversity of education. A general state education is a mere contrivance for molding people to be exactly like one another: and as the mold in which it casts them is that which pleases the predominant power . . . or the majority of the existing generation, in proportion as it is efficient and successful, it establishes a despotism over the mind, leading by natural tendency to one over the body.[21]

Mill went on to say that state education "should only exist, if it exists at all, as one among many competing experiments, carried on for the purpose of example and stimulus, to keep the others up to a certain standard of excellence." Ideally, he wrote, government's role in education should be confined to the payment of fees for what he called "the poorer classes."

The initial reaction of a twenty-first-century American to such proposals is apt to be: "Wouldn't educational diversity of the type Mill advocated worsen economic and social divisions among our highly heterogeneous population? And what about religious schools where the teaching would be explicitly antiliberal?"[22] Those are serious questions. There is no denying that those risks exist, just as there is no pretending that the answers are clear. But since we in the United States have established the very system that Mill considered most dangerous, should we not give some attention to the risks about which he warned? With government firmly in control of and religion largely banned from the majority of our nation's chief institutions for teaching and transmitting culture, what is the likely effect upon our country's ability to form citizens with the habits and attitudes that a liberal democracy requires?

Since the present symposium was held under the auspices of the James Madison Program, it seems appropriate to recall that Madison himself acknowledged in *Federalist* 55 that republican government requires a higher degree of virtue in its citizens than any other form. The idea that our democratic experiment requires certain habits, skills, and attitudes on the part of citizens and statespersons is a proposition shared, I believe, by a broad range of thinkers that would include Richard Neuhaus, Robert George, William Galston, and Steven Macedo.

Probably broad agreement could also be reached at the general level about the qualities that a liberal polity requires. Self-government requires certain civic skills (deliberation, compromise, consensus-building, civility, reason-giving) as well as theaters where those skills can be exercised. Ordered liberty requires citizens who are independent of mind, public-spirited, respectful of the rule of law, capable of self-restraint, aware of their rights, and respectful of the rights of others. The egalitarian and welfare aspirations to which we have committed ourselves in modern times require an even higher degree of civic virtue: a modicum of fellow-feeling as well as a certain disposition to assume responsibility for oneself and one's dependents.

Where disagreement emerges is less about the qualities that are required than about how and by whom they should be fostered and the role of religion in fostering them. Here we have what may well be the central domestic political problem of our time: How can we assure a continuing supply of citizens and statespersons who can "reflect soberly, deliberate well, and choose dispassionately and justly on the merits of the case under consideration, in such a way that others can count on our commitment and our long-term purpose"?[23] What can or should we do to instill the skills, habits, and virtues required for the survival and flourishing of free, democratic institutions in a pluralistic society?

The challenge is a formidable one. In fact, the classical political philosophers doubted that democracy could survive in an extended territory with a heterogeneous population. Madison and his contemporaries were well aware that the experiment they were launching defied the wisdom of the ancients. Madison in *The Federalist* stated his confidence that his fellow citizens were up to the job, but even he declined to speculate about future years when the country might become larger and more heterogeneous.[24]

Twenty-five years ago, in the wake of the cultural revolution of the 1960s and 1970s, Richard Neuhaus correctly saw that the chief threat to our republic was not communism (as many thought at the time) but "a collapse of the idea of freedom and of the social arrangements necessary to sustaining liberal democracy."[25] That problem also worried William Galston, who wrote in 1993 that the American experiment "is in trouble because it has failed to attend to the dependence of sound politics on sound culture."[26] The liberal state, he contended, must become "far more actively involved in reproducing the conditions necessary to its own health and perpetuation," but it must do so without undermining "the capacious tolerance that gives liberal society its special attraction."

Like the intrepid hero of *The Terminator*, Neuhaus wanted to increase the likelihood that future Americans would rise to the challenges ahead. With hindsight, however, it seems to me that Neuhaus, uncharacteristically, held back from following his own train of thought to its natural conclusion. Though he mentioned in passing the "lethal liberationisms that reached their frenzied apex in the late sixties and early seventies,"[27] he did not explore what that social revolution was doing to the cultural foundations of our republic. Twenty-five years later, it now seems clear that those years of adult "liberation" took a dreadful toll on children and on the nation's principal seedbeds of character and competence—families and their surrounding communities of memory and mutual aid.

Neuhaus was fond of saying that Americans are "incorrigibly religious." And in at least some sense surely they are. But in our increasingly secular society what many Americans now seem to want is for *other people* to be "incorrigibly religious" (or at least to behave as if they were). They want other people to cultivate the self-restraint that makes social life possible, other people to hang in there when family life gets tough, other people to be ethical in business dealings, other people to pay taxes, and other people to provide children with attention and discipline. While Neuhaus was urging free citizens to claim their rightful places in public life, we were becoming a nation of free riders, coasting along on a dwindling social capital. At the same time our spaces for civic engagement have been shrinking, the country has also been losing many of the associations and institutions where republican skills and virtues are generated, regenerated, nurtured, and transmitted from one generation to the next.

Perhaps it would not have suited the upbeat mood of *The Naked Public Square* to dwell on the state of American culture. The book, after all, was a rallying cry. But on the very last page, Neuhaus observed that the "new thing we are looking for may not come at all. The naked public square may be the last phase of a failed experiment." No doubt he meant that warning as a spur to action. Today it has a more ominous sound.

3

The Naked European Constitution

J. H. H. Weiler

I

In the process of drafting the so-called European Constitution, there were repeated attempts, supported by the late Pope John Paul II, to include in its preamble an *invocatio Dei* (such as found, for example, in the German constitution) or a reference to Europe's Christian roots (such as found in the constitutions of many member states of the European Union). These attempts failed. At the final horse-trading session among the governments of the member states of the European Union, even those governments which had supported the inclusion caved in. The final document put before the European peoples had but an anodyne reference to "the cultural, religious and humanist inheritance of Europe."

Those anguished by this outcome, have seen it as a symptom of Europe's turning away from its Christian "roots," and as a sign of the rampant secularization of European societies. It is also regarded by many as a symbol of everything that is wrong with the Union and the notion of European integration itself.

Those who opposed a constitutional reference to God or Christianity justified such opposition in the name of a new and better Europe represented by the Union, which was more multicultural and tolerant. They also justified such opposition as reflecting an appropriate constitutional position of and for Europe—one which guaranteed freedom of religion but according to which the "State" had to be above any expression of religious preferences. To include a reference to God or Christianity would constitute an unacceptable signal of constitutional intolerance—a betrayal of the ideals of the European Union.

In this essay, I do not want to argue from a religious perspective but adopt instead the very same pluralist-democratic and constitutional premises which at least seemed to underlie the principled opposition to the *invocatio Dei*. Based on these premises, I will contend that it is the rejection of a reference to God and/or Christianity in the preamble of the constitution which represents true constitutional intolerance and a betrayal of the deepest ideals of European integration and the Union.

At some level, the matter may now appear academic. The constitution perished with a resounding rejection by the electorates of France and the Netherlands. The Dutch and French results reflect something more than an aberrational and idiosyncratic choice in two member states. The Spanish referendum was distinguished by a large majority and small turnout, so small that in Italy the result would be considered constitutionally invalid. The massive Ceaușescu-like votes in several national parliaments hardly reflected similar sentiment in their own public piazzas. And it is likely that had the process of ratification not been hastily aborted, there would have been some rejections and some very close votes in several of the other member states scheduled for a referendum. Ultimately, my assessment is that a majority of European citizens in a majority of member states would have given their support to the constitution had the process taken its course, but still far from the kind of majority which would bestow legitimacy on a constitution. A constitution rejected (in all likelihood) by two founding member states, by at least two of the large member states (if we assume as one safely can that the United Kingdom would have voted "no" and the Poles quite likely too), and probably by one or more of the new member states is not one that could be said to enjoy the kind of legitimacy which those who advocated the shift from Europe's "common law" constitution to a formal document had imagined and hoped for.

It would be tempting to argue that one reason which accounts for this public rejection was the failure to make reference to Europe's Christian roots. I doubt this argument can be sustained in this robust version. But it cannot be excluded as a symptomatic factor in the evident breakdown of trust between the European elites, who almost universally supported the document (it was endorsed by all twenty-five governments!), and by very broad sections of European public opinion. This was a veritable "Revolt of the Masses."

For a long time, I have been in an uncomfortable position, being one of those rather few Euro-Constitutionalists who publicly and repeatedly called into question the need for, and the wisdom of, the formal constitutional project. Europe's basic common-law constitutional architecture, I argued, was not only functionally sound, but also noble and original, fashioned in accordance with Schuman's astute step-by-step approach in a remarkable consensual "multilogue" among Europe's courts and other public actors, high and low. This collaborative judicial-political exercise was not only procedurally expedient, it was a reflection of Europe's substantive Grundnorm (its basic constitutional norm) and its most striking contribution to transnational statecraft: the principle of constitutional tolerance. What is more, the constitutional architecture enjoyed a high index of political and legal legitimacy, ratified repeatedly by all member states' parliaments in accordance with their constitutional provisions through regular intergovernmental conferences and treaty revisions. The new constitution was a slide to banality, I argued, motivated by hubris.

The debate which unfolded in this constitutional saga about Christian roots involved more than the traditional battleground trying to demarcate the borders between church and state. It was a debate about the shaping of Europe's self-understanding and self-definition of its identity. It offers an interesting and sobering view of Europe's current constitutional moment.

II

How Christian is Europe? Christianity, as understood by itself, is revealed Truth. A universal truth. It is the normative word of God, a guide for an ordered life in this world and the means for salvation in the next.

Christianity is, too, an empirical social reality, a community of persons who think of themselves as Christian with different levels of commitment to normative Christianity. In its "thick" social version, it is a community of believers for whom Christian identity is of very important significance in their self-understanding and who attempt to follow the practices and teachings of their church. Both Church and church play appreciable roles in their daily lives and, notably, in the education they give and the hopes they have for their children. In its "thin" social version, it is composed of people who would think of themselves as being Christian but to whom that facet of their identity is not at the forefront. Their Christian "practice" will manifest itself in, notably, the vital moments of life—birth, marriage, death. If Catholic, they may attend Mass infrequently and Communion hardly at all (since it involves confession), and not partake in any active way in the life of either church or Church. But they would still be married in the Church, would want to see their kids baptized, and would be horrified to think that their death would be without any religious sacrament and ministry of God.

Christianity as cultus, conditioned by that which we worship or worshipped in the past, is, finally, a manifestation of, and vehicle and repository for, elements of what we think of as our culture: culture in the narrower sense of our aesthetic sensibilities as expressed in the arts such as literature, poetry, music, paint-

ing, and sculpture, but also culture in a broader sense capturing
our universe of values and moral sensibilities—our political and
social culture.

Now let me move on to the obvious. I have always found
evocative the story in Numbers 13 and Deuteronomy 1 of the
men who were sent to tour the Promised Land: *mitte viros qui
considerent terram Chanaan*! In the Hebrew text the verb is
Turu—the original tourists! Imagine, then, several such tourists
sent to explore the Promised Land of Europe. Let us have them
land, say, in Palermo and travel north, traversing Italy, Austria,
and Slovenia into Germany, and then have some continue north
to the Scandinavian countries, others turn west into the Low-
lands and through France to the Iberian peninsula, and yet others explore the lands which constitute what was until recently
Eastern Europe.

What would they report back? They would talk of a rather
small continent with a rich and enticing Babel of different
peoples with different identities in different lands, with different topographies and different climates, speaking different languages, telling different stories and histories (sometimes of the
very same events), boasting different cultural achievements, and
each swearing that their food (or at least coffee, or schnapps, or
bread) is the best, that their lakes (or sea, or sky, or mountains,
or, yes, women, or language) are the most beautiful, and each
determined to preserve that very special identity.

"Where is 'Europe'?" we might ask, in this Babel of differences?

After a pause our tourists would, no doubt, mention the won-
ders of the European common marketplace, which allows these
different peoples to wear very similar clothes (usually made in
China), use very similar gadgets and appliances (made in Japan,
Taiwan, and Korea), watch the same movies (made, *quelle hor-
reur*, in the United States), and fall asleep to very similar TV
shows with almost identical publicity spots (made—yes!—in
Europe). Our tourists might not know Polish or German or Por-

tuguese, but after a visit to those countries, they will be in no doubt as to the laundry soap which washes whitest.

But in the search for "Europe" they would, too, recount the following: that in every single habitation, even the smallest, the graves in the cemeteries might carry inscriptions in the different European languages, but the overwhelming majority also carry the very same Christian cross; that, at least in the Europe of the West, there is no town or village of an appreciable size which does not have at least one, and sometimes many more, Christian churches. In some places these churches might be very empty most days of the year, but there they stand—often in glorious beauty, often dominating the very center of the public space. Our tourists would come across some synagogues (and had the visit taken place before 1939, a lot more) and some mosques as well as Jewish and Muslim cemeteries. They, too, are an integral part of the European landscape but numerically far smaller, bringing into even sharper relief the predominantly Christian contours of Europe.

The tourists would speak of different social realities of the Christians: In some countries, the tourists would find vibrant and large communities of practicing Christians—sometimes the majority of the population. In other countries, such expression of "thick" Christian reality would have dwindled. Many churches would stand empty, deconsecrated, sometimes sold and used as shopping malls, the new shrines to Mammon. But in all European countries, with no exception, a large majority of the population belong at least to that second group, of vital-moments Christians.

"And culture?" we might ask. We do not need the tourists to tell us that story. The Christian influence on our European culture is simply overwhelming. The evidence is all around—in architecture, in (mostly classical) music, and in the plastic arts as well as in literature and poetry. Not surprising, of course. That which we worship becomes almost naturally the object for expressing our most creative and inspired efforts. The historical dominance of Christian influence has produced an exquisite dialectical effect whereby much art which is not Christian was produced in opposition to it and, is, thus, inextricably linked to it and cannot be understood outside of that context. That is true, even more so, in the realm of political culture, in the realm of ideas and of values. European moral sensibilities are conditioned by this Christian heritage and, in recent times, by the struggles with it.

"Europe" is not only an empirical reality. It is, too, an idea, an ideal—a project for a better polity and society. Europe's idea and ideal is to be more than a coalition of market interests and an interest in a free market. It is also committed to more than some minimal universal normativity, as evidenced by the European Convention of Human Rights (ECHR). If that were not so, why would it not content itself with a Free Trade Area Agreement coupled with membership in the Council of Europe and the ECHR? Europe aspires to be an ethical community. Europe claims a specificity, an identity which is to be understood exactly with the vocabulary of the ethical community. And, just as democracy is premised on the existence of demos (however defined), community and identity are premised on the existence of memory, which is to say, history.

What is Europe's history, without which it can have no identity, no tale around which to coalesce, no ethos, and no telos? Like beauty, it is, of course, in the eye of the beholder. What we privilege in this narrative will depend on who is doing the narration. It is a story of progress and regress, of great scientific and cultural development, but also of the horrible things Europeans did to each other and to others beyond the Continent. But in this story, which is as integral and indispensable to the idea and identity of Europe as are its natural and human resources, Christianity has had an ever present and oft critical role. Europeans were thrown to the lions and they threw to the lions. Some will want to emphasize this and some will want to emphasize that. There are glorious Christian moments in this story, and there are shameful moments. But one can no more airbrush Christianity out of Europe's history, ancient and contemporary, than one could knock off all those crosses in the graveyards of Europe.

I often make believe that on the masthead of the famous British weekly magazine *The Economist* is found the motto "Simplify and Exaggerate!" If, then, one of our tourists were an editor of *The Economist*, the title of his travelogue would be "Europe Is Christian!" Simple, banal, and not very nuanced, but containing an important truth. A more prudent reporter, writing perhaps for *Le Monde Diplomatique*, might say that by at least one of the ways of understanding Christianity and oftentimes by more than one, even today a major component of Europe's makeup is Christian. This, too, would be stating the obvious (the obvious to some is more impressive when stated in a prolix sentence), which brings us right to the gates of the European Christian Ghetto.

This ghetto is surrounded by external and internal walls. The external walls represent an attitude which in my view can be well encapsulated by the term Christophobia. Not simply a "principled" constitutional notion of secularism, it is a powerful negative animus toward Christianity. The internal walls reflect a certain internalization by practicing Christians of a prevalent constitutional dogma: religion—the protection of which comes under the rubric of freedom of conscience—is a matter of private belief, the only appropriate place for which is outside of the public piazza.

Two anecdotal events may serve as perfect metaphors for the external and internal walls of the European Christian Ghetto. The first is very well known: the refusal, first by the Convention which drafted the European Charter of Fundamental Human Rights, and then by the Convention which drafted the European Constitution, to include a reference to, an allusion to, or a mere mention of Christianity in the respective preambles of these two documents.

The second anecdote is, in my eyes, more evocative and more consequential. Three or four years ago, I pulled from the library of my university all of the books it contained dealing generally with the European Union and European integration published in the past year or so.[1] These were books discussing the nature of European integration, its future, its theory, or its general orientation. All in all, I gathered eighty-six books. I know the authors of quite a few of these books. I know some to be practicing Christians. And yet, in seventy-nine of the eighty-six books, there was not a single allusion or reference to Christianity. Why, after all, should there be? The European Union is the shared public square of Europe.

The Americans speak of a "wall of separation" between church and state against which you often find the faithful of various religions aiming their battering rams. Here, however, to judge from the literature of and on the European Union, was a self-imposed "wall of separation."

To the extent that these two anecdotes represent a reality, Christian thinking and European integration seem to be moving in mutually exclusive spheres. Until the clarion call of the late John Paul II, Christianity did not figure on the radar of the European Union and the process of European integration; likewise, it would seem, with a few notable exceptions (for example the current pope), that it did not figure in any serious way on the Christian radar.

III

A Charter of Rights for Europe was an idea that had been around for at least twenty-five years. There is some tedium in recounting this saga, but it repays some study. In 1989, it actually happened. The European Charter of Fundamental Human Rights was debated, negotiated, and drafted by a new kind of body—a convention meant to represent the peoples of Europe rather than the habitual diplomatic mandarins. A slightly bloated body composed of representatives of the governments of the member states, of the parliaments of the member states, of the European Parliament, and of the other European institutions of governance met for a year and produced the Charter.

Strange as it may sound to those not familiar with these matters, there was no compelling functional reason for the exercise. After all, the citizens of Europe appear to "suffer" from a surfeit rather than a deficit of judicial protection of their fundamental rights, protected as they are by national constitutions and national courts, by the safety net provided by the European Convention of Human Rights, and by the European Court of Justice of the European Union, which since at least 1969 has purported to guarantee that Community measures violating fundamental human rights which form part of the common constitutional tradition of the member states are unacceptable and would be struck down. One should absolutely not gain the impression that without the Charter, the fundamental rights of European citizens are not being protected. This is simply not the case.

So why a new charter at all? Most important in the eyes of the Charter promoters was the issue of perception and identity. In recent years the political legitimacy of the European construct has been a live issue; the advent of the European Monetary Union with its barely accountable European Central Bank has added fuel to a perception of a Europe concerned more with markets than with people. It may be true that the European Court guarantees legal protection against human rights abuses, but who was aware of this? A Charter, its supporters said, would render visible and prominent that which until now was known only to dusty lawyers.

The Charter, is, thus, an important symbol counterbalancing the Euro and the economic dimension of Europe, a part of the constitutional iconography of European integration, contributing appreciably to its self-understanding as a community of values and hence to its articulation of its identity.

Several delegates to the Convention which drafted the Charter requested that its preamble include some reference to Christianity, to the Judeo-Christian tradition, or, eventually, simply to the religious heritage of Europe. As is well known, all three requests were rejected. The "compromise" (if that is what a wholesale capitulation can be called) refers instead to Europe's "spiritual and moral heritage."

One may wonder why, in the context of a Charter of fundamental rights, a request was made to include a reference to the Christian and eventually to the religious heritage of Europe. Was this not a simple provocation? After all, the Charter itself does protect freedom of religion. Is that not enough?

So the question emerged whether the request to include a reference to the religious heritage was justified. That is how many at the convention approached the issue.

Those who believe that inclusion is justified would be tempted at this point to offer not one justification but a long list. But it is important to note the subtle sleight of hand in the question itself. Why should one have to justify the inclusion? Why should the onus not be on those seeking to justify the rejection? This point is not some adolescent argumentative point. Throughout public life the question as to who has the onus of justification is a valuable Geiger detector of social presumptions and, frequently, of societal biases. Examples abound: Classically, in our criminal law system, a defendant does not have to prove his innocence; it is assumed. The prosecution has to prove the defendant's guilt. If the defendant had to prove his innocence, the assumption would be that he is guilty absent such proof. Here is another example: Historically, in their fight for emancipation, women had to prove every step of the way their eligibility for the vote, for public office, for certain jobs, etc. The presumption was that absent that proof and justification, women were inferior.

If one has to justify the inclusion of a religious reference, this would suggest that presumptively the European public space is a secular environment. Whether that is so or should be so is an issue which requires careful consideration, and one should not jump to facile conclusions. After all, the constitutional and civic traditions in many member states point to variations on this theme, many of which point to an opposite conclusion.

It is, thus, perhaps better, instead of asking whether the inclusion of a reference to religion in the preamble to the charter would have been and would be justified, to ask for the reasons which may have prompted the request in the first place.

What, then, prompts the request? Simply reading the preamble as originally drafted offers many answers.

Preamble

The peoples of Europe, in creating an ever closer union among them, are resolved to share a peaceful future based on common values.

Conscious of its spiritual and moral heritage, the Union is founded on the indivisible, universal values of human dignity, freedom, equality and solidarity; it is based on the principles of democracy and the rule of law. It places the individual at the heart of its activities, by establishing the citizenship of the Union and by creating an area of freedom, security and justice.

The Union contributes to the preservation and to the development of these common values while respecting the diversity of the cultures and traditions of the peoples of Europe as well as the national identities of the Member States and the organisation of their public authorities at national, regional and local levels; it seeks to promote balanced and sustainable development and ensures free movement of persons, goods, services and capital, and the freedom of establishment.

To this end, it is necessary to strengthen the protection of fundamental rights in the light of changes in society, social progress and scientific and technological developments by making those rights more visible in a Charter.

This Charter reaffirms, with due regard for the powers and tasks of the Community and the Union and the principle of subsidiarity, the rights as they result, in particular, from the constitutional traditions and international obligations common to the Member States, the Treaty on European Union, the Community Treaties, the European Convention for the Protection of Human Rights and Fundamental Freedoms, the Social Charters adopted by the Community and by the Council of Europe and the case-law of the Court of Justice of the European Communities and of the European Court of Human Rights.

Enjoyment of these rights entails responsibilities and duties with regard to other persons, to the human community and to future generations.

The Union therefore recognises the rights, freedoms and principles set out hereafter.

Evidently the stakes are high. This is not a technical preamble to some day-to-day legislation. Indeed, the opening paragraphs could serve just as well as a preamble to a full-fledged constitution and not simply as one preceding the Charter of Fundamental Human Rights. In fact, the original idea of the Charter was that it would constitute a first element in a future constitution for Europe.

This, of course, became doubly so for the draft Constitution. Both preambles constituted a primordial articulation of Europe's constitutional self-understanding—of what it is about and of what it stands for.

Europe very appropriately defines itself as, inter alia, a community of values. What goes in and what is left out matters. It matters in and of itself—as values should. It also matters if Europe is to elicit the kind of affective commitment which is the basis for a meaningful polity. People need to see themselves, their better part, reflected in such a self-understanding. And if we are part of a pluralist society and believe in the virtue of such pluralism and tolerance, we must accept that such self-understandings reflect that pluralism.

It is not, thus, surprising, given the high symbolic and affective stakes, that in both conventions, which distanced themselves from the traditional diplomatic, secretive, and elitist European modus operandi and which prided themselves on their democratic and populist sensibility, many delegates requested a reference to Christianity in the preamble. They were simply reflecting the preferences of those whom they represented. Religion, after all, constitutes an important dimension in the self-understanding of a huge number of people in Europe. If Europe is to be their Europe too, it might have appeared natural to them that the preamble would contain some allusion to that important dimension of their lives, to their perception of an important element of Europe's makeup. This is sometimes called democracy.

But beyond the generic wish to see oneself reflected—included—in that which is meant to be the collective mirror, there was a specificity to the request in the context of both the preamble of the Constitution and the preamble of the Charter of Fundamental Human Rights. This is a hugely important point: the constitution, the charter, and Europe itself become more meaningful to those it is meant to serve if it can be integrated into their worldview (without, of course, giving undue offense to others).

There is a way in which the religious in general and Christians more specifically may interpret the very telos of these projects. (Note: it is *a* way, not *the* way.)

IV

Let me first illustrate such an understanding in relation to the idea of Europe as a whole and then more specifically in relation to the charter.

Peace, in the immediate wake of World War II, was the most explicit and evocative objective for which the would-be polity was an instrument. Nowhere is this captured better than in the oft repeated phraseology of the Schuman Declaration of May 9, 1950:

> World peace cannot be safeguarded without the making of constructive efforts proportionate to the dangers which threaten it. . . .
>
> The gathering of the nations of Europe requires the elimination of the age-old opposition of France and the Federal Republic of Germany. The first concern in any action undertaken must be these two countries. . . .
>
> [This] solidarity . . . will make it plain that any war between France and the Federal Republic of Germany becomes, not merely unthinkable, but materially impossible.

Peace, at all times an attractive desideratum, would have had its appeal in purely instrumental and utilitarian terms. But it is readily apparent that in the historical context in which the Schuman Plan was put forward, the notion of peace as an ideal probes a far deeper stratum than simple swords into plough-shares, sitting under one's vines and fig trees, lambs lying with wolves—the classic biblical metaphors for peace. The dilemma posed was an acute example of the alleged tension between grace and justice which has taxed philosophers and theologians through the ages—from William of Ockham (premodern) to Friedrich Nietzsche (modernist) to the repugnant but profound Martin Heidegger (postmodern).

These were, after all, the early 1950s with the horrors of war still fresh in the mind and, in particular, the memory of the unspeakable savagery of German occupation. It would take many years for the hatred in countries such as the Netherlands, Denmark, and France to subside fully. The idea, then, in 1950, of a community of equals as providing the structural underpinning for long-term peace among yesteryear's enemies represented more than the wise counsel of experienced statesmen.

It was a call, therefore, not only for "peace" of the external, international-relations type that one finds, for example, in the Charter of the United Nations, but also for internal peace, for forgiveness, a challenge to overcome an understandable hatred. In that particular historical context, the European notion of peace resonates with and is evocative of the distinct discourse, imagery, and values of Christian Love, of Grace—not, I think, a particularly astonishing evocation given the personal backgrounds of the Founding Fathers: Adenauer, De Gaspari, Schuman, Monnet himself.

So, when the new constitution speaks of the determination of "the peoples of Europe . . . to transcend their ancient divisions and, united ever more closely, to forge a common destiny," or when the Charter speaks of "[t]he peoples of Europe . . . creating an ever closer union among them, . . . resolved to share a peaceful future based on common values," it was not inappropriate for those who wished to integrate that message of integration into their Christian worldview to seek an overt acknowledgment. Was it appropriate to have refused? In the same way that we had to explain the request, we will have to attempt to explain the refusal. Christianity has no monopoly over the ideas of love and peace (though its teaching is very special and striking), and others could integrate this central message of Europe into their respective worldviews; likewise, the request was not to make the allusion to Christianity the exclusive reference in the preamble to the Constitution. But at least at this point the different approaches do not seem mutually exclusive—hence our puzzlement over the refusal. It becomes even more puzzling in the context of the Charter, where the request was eventually boiled down to a simple allusion to the generic phrase "religious heritage."

The preamble defines the basic nexus among the peoples of Europe as one based on common values, notably the "universal values of human dignity, freedom, equality and solidarity . . . the principles of democracy and the rule of law and the placing of . . . the individual at the heart of [the Union's] activities." Here we are touching the defining core of what used to be called Western liberal democracies. These are some of the values which are meant to enlist our constitutional patriotism. It is important not only to proclaim these values but also to believe in them and, hopefully, to practice them.

Commitment can come from different cognitive and epistemic sources. Why exclude a commitment that comes from the religious worldview? In this context it would be appropriate to make use of that much abused term, the Judeo-Christian tradition. For those who belong to that tradition, the wellspring of the commitment to human rights finds its best expression in the majestic Genesis 1:27: "So God created man in his own image, in the image of God created he him; male and female created he them."

This is a verse whose profound relevance to the notions of dignity and equality requires no exegesis. Additionally, there is, inadvertently of course, something very "European" in this verse from Genesis. Within the Western liberal tradition there are significant nuances and differences in the articulation of and sensibility toward fundamental human rights. One notable distinction of both symbolic and practical import is between the American emphasis in their universe of human rights on liberty and the European emphasis on dignity. Genesis privileges dignity by referring to man and woman as created in the image of God. A more potent nuance is to be found in relation to freedom. For the religious worldview, freedom is not unbounded and must be part of a discipline of ethical truth.

There are, of course, other profoundly serious ways in which a commitment to human rights can be rooted in a secular worldview, such as the liberal neo-Kantian approach. And the secular worldview has its own take on liberty, such as theories of rational liberty and the rule of law. On these issues the secular and the religious worldviews do not lead to mutually exclusive results, which makes it even harder to understand the exclusion.

The very preamble of the Charter speaks of the contribution of Europe to "the preservation and to the development of these common values while respecting the diversity of the cultures and traditions of the peoples of Europe."

It is an odd way to respect the diversity of cultures and traditions by excluding any reference to one of the most salient and common such cultures. Is the deliberate exclusion to be understood as a statement that religion generally and Christianity in particular are inimical to human rights? Some, I know, may think just that. But be that as it may, it is simply self-defeating to expunge a reference to that which makes the very project of Europe and the project of human rights more meaningful to a large number of those for whom these projects are designed.

What, then, explains this adamant rejection of any reference to Christianity in the constitutional documents of the Union?

V

How does one explain the intensity of the resistance toward all things religious and Christian in the European construct? My argument here is somewhat complex, so it may be helpful to outline first its structure and then follow with the full elaboration.

The reason most commonly given in the context of the European debate is of a constitutional nature: it would, it is argued, be constitutionally inappropriate for there to be an explicit reference to Christianity. I will argue first that there is no compelling constitutional reason to oppose a reference to Christianity in the preambles, and that this is even more the case in the European context. Let us say, however, that I am wrong, that there is some valid constitutional reason to oppose a reference to Christianity in the preambles of the Charter and of the Constitution. Even those who hold such a view would, I will argue, have to concede that it is at best a close case, and not a particularly powerful one. And yet the opposition to inclusion was extremely ferocious and insistent. Ultimately, all compromises were rejected: Christianity was excluded.

The discrepancy between the weak constitutional argument and the ferocity of opposition lead me to speculate that the constitutional reason, whatever its merit, cannot explain the full set of motives of those opposed. My thesis is that in large measure there are other motives which drive those opponents and that the constitutional argument is simply used to present in a principled way that which is driven by deeper sociological and psychological reasons. Note, I am not arguing a lack of good faith. The people opposed will, in most cases, make the constitutional argument in good faith. But in my view, this alone cannot explain their full set of motives. For these we have to probe deeper in an inquiry that by necessity will be speculative and approximate, and that will present a multifaceted set of non-mutually-exclusive motives, some or all of which can be held simultaneously. I will, as indicated above, call this ensemble the European Christophobia.

Finally, I will argue that the community of the Christian faithful also plays a role in this story—in part by contributing to a certain politicization of an issue which should be nonpartisan, and in part, as I shall explain below in discussing the "internal walls" of the ghetto, by remaining silent in the engagement between Christianity and Europe.

Let us first map the constitutional terrain and try to do it in a way that is both interesting and comprehensible to readers who are not constitutionalists. These issues are, after all, too important to leave in the hands of lawyers.

There is, first, a classic, constitutionally significant debate about the proper relationship between church and state. The constitutional premise for such a debate in Europe (and beyond) is a common belief that the constitutional order should protect both freedom *of* religion and freedom *from* religion. To live within the European constitutional order broadly defined is to live in a legal space which guarantees to the religiously inclined the freedom to practice their religion, and to those who are secular, freedom from any religious coercion. All member states of the European Union, under the umbrella of the European Convention of Human Rights, share this constitutional premise.

Even if there is the broad constitutional consensus, there is much difference in its application in the various member states. There will, of course, be borderline cases (which lawyers just love): What is to count as a religion for the purposes of constitutional protection? Is, for example, Scientology to be recognized as a religion whose adherents may enjoy these guarantees? European constitutional courts, though sharing the constitutional premise, may differ on this question. There are, too, in this case, as in other cases of fundamental rights guaranteed by the constitutional order, limits. If a recognized religion required of its adherents human sacrifice, we would surely not, in the name of freedom of religion, guarantee the right to such a rite (even if the would-be victim consented to his or her sacrifice). Sometimes the limits will not be as obvious. If it turns out that the Jewish and Muslim ritual slaughter (kosher/hallal) is cruel to animals (something that is hotly disputed), could it be banned, or should freedom of religion prevail? And we are all aware of the difficult decisions faced in relation to the Muslim veil or the Sikh turban. Is there a compelling state interest which would justify banning the wearing of such foulards in public schools (though they be religiously mandated) or the wearing of turbans by Sikh police? Again, different constitutional courts, though sharing the constitutional premise of freedom of religion and freedom from religion, might come to different conclusions. The extant European constitutional architecture already embraces the constitutional premise. The Union regards itself as being bound by the relevant material provisions of the European Convention on Human Rights and by the constitutional traditions common to its member states, religious freedom being one such common tradition. Article 10 of the new Charter and Article 51 of the draft Constitution confirm this preexisting commitment.

VI

All of the individual member states as well as the corporate Union are, then, as we have seen, committed to the notions of freedom of religion and freedom from religion (though there is a margin of autonomy allowing different solutions to some of the borderline cases explained above). There is, however, a second delicate constitutional issue which brings us closer to the current debate. A constitution is not just a list of guaranteed rights of individuals and groups vis-à-vis public authority. And it is not only a set of rules regulating as a matter of "higher law" the structure and processes of governance. It is, too, a repository of important elements which define our collective identity as nations and as ethical communities. National constitutions will, typically, contain a part that is a reflection of European and universal values, but they will also contain a part that is a reflection of the specific and particular. Universality and particularity both play important parts in a constitution. Europe has now adopted as its motto "United in Diversity." Diversity also finds its expression in our constitutions. Otherwise, we would all have the same constitution, simply written in different languages.

To what extent, then, may the constitution make reference to religion, to God, or to Christianity if it is thought that such reference is an important part of, say, the cultural and/or historical and/or political identity of the very people whom the constitution constitutes? In at least some way the most compelling answer to this question is empirical. While all member states of the European Union are committed to freedom of and from religion, to this question they give very, very different answers.

We have at one extreme the French *laique* constitutional understanding, expressed in the terse preamble to its current (1958) constitution, making a reference to the majestic declaration of 1789:

Le peuple français proclame solennellement son attachement aux Droits de l'homme et aux principes de la souver-

aineté nationale tels qu'ils ont été définis par la Déclara-
tion de 1789, confirmée et complétée par le préambule de
la Constitution de 1946.

You will search in vain to find any religious or transcendental
allusion. It is proudly secular, rooted as it is in the historical anti-
clericalism of the French Revolution. Article 1 of the French constitution specifically defines the Republic as *laique*.

Compare this now to the preamble to the Irish constitution:

> In the Name of the Most Holy Trinity, from Whom is all
> authority and to Whom, as our final end, all actions both
> of men and States must be referred, We, the people of Éire,
> Humbly acknowledging all our obligations to our Divine
> Lord, Jesus Christ, Who sustained our fathers through
> centuries of trial, Gratefully remembering their heroic and
> unremitting struggle to regain the rightful independence
> of our Nation, And seeking to promote the common good,
> with due observance of Prudence, Justice and Charity, so
> that the dignity and freedom of the individual may be
> assured, true social order attained, the unity of our coun-
> try restored, and concord established with other nations,
> Do hereby adopt, enact, and give to ourselves this Con-
> stitution.

One can go even further: just as integral to the European
constitutional tradition are those member states which, while
guaranteeing freedom of religion and freedom from religion,
have, nonetheless an "established" state church.

This from the Danish constitution:

> The Evangelical Lutheran Church shall be the Established
> Church of Denmark, and, as such, it shall be supported by
> the State . . .

And this from the Greek constitution:

Article 3(1) The prevailing religion in Greece is that of the Eastern Orthodox Church of Christ. The Orthodox Church of Greece acknowledging as its head Our Lord Jesus Christ is indissolubly united in doctrine with the Great Church of Constantinople and every other Church of Christ of the same doctrine. It observes steadfastly, as they do, the holy apostolic and synodical canons and the holy tradition. It is autocephalous, exercising its sovereign rights independently of any other church, and is administered by the Holy Synod of Bishops and the Parliament Holy Synod which emanates from the former and is constituted in accordance with the Constitutional Charter of the Church and the provisions of the Patriarchal Document of 29 June 1850 and the Synodal Deed of 4 September 1928. (2) The religious status prevailing in certain parts of the State is not contrary to the provisions of the aforegoing paragraph. (3) The text of the Holy Scriptures shall be maintained unaltered. The official translation thereof into any other linguistic form, without the sanction of the Autocephalous Church of Greece and the Great Church of Christ in Constantinople, is prohibited.

And a more attenuated position in Spain—on the one hand a very robust protection of the freedom of religion:

Section 16: (1) Freedom of ideology, religion and worship of individuals and communities is guaranteed, with no other restriction on their expression than may be necessary to maintain public order as protected by law. (2) No one may be compelled to make statements regarding his or her ideology, religion or beliefs. . . .

Then, on the other hand, while rejecting an established church such as we find in Denmark or Britain, where the head of state is the head of the church, the Spanish constitution accords a privileged mention to the Roman Catholic Church: "(3) No religion shall have a state character. The public authorities shall take into account the religious beliefs of Spanish society and shall consequently maintain appropriate cooperative relations with the Catholic Church and other confessions."

And with these examples I have not exhausted the constitutional permutations in Europe.

How does one reconcile, constitutionally, these positions? Who is right? The French, who studiously exclude all transcendental or religious reference (even though the majority of the French population is religious and certainly was at the time their constitution was adopted), or the Germans with their generic reference to God? The Irish or the Spanish, with their most parochial and explicit references? Or, perhaps, those like the Danes, the Greeks, and the British who have some form of state religion?

The answer is that there is no need to reconcile these approaches, for they give empirical expression to two important features of the European constitutional architecture. The first reflects an important part of the European constitutional settlement in the matter of church and state, which is to say, a common understanding of the basic premise of freedom of and from religion coupled with a common understanding that that premise is not violated by the mere fact that a constitution gives expression to the religious or *laique* sensibility of the polity in its preambular provisions or even as an established religion. If, having been inspired by, say, the Irish preamble, public authorities in Ireland were to engage in religious coercion of secular citizens and residents, they may be found (even formally by the ECHR court) to violate the principle of freedom from religion. Likewise, if inspired by their *laique* ethos, French public authorities engaged in unjustified restrictions on religious practices, they might be in violation of the principle of freedom of religion. But, in and of themselves, neither the Irish preamble nor the Danish or Greek or Spanish and other similar provisions are considered to be a violation of the constitutional commitment to religious freedom and tolerance.

The second constitutional feature is the matter of diversity. Europe is diverse not only in its languages and culture but also in its constitutional and political cultures. Part of French specificity, part of French identity is reflected in, say, their gorgeous rich language as well as in their *laique* constitutional tradition. Part of Irish identity is reflected in their literary and poetic heritage—so distinct a voice in the English-speaking world—and, yes, in their religious constitutional vocabulary. This constitutional heterogeneity is to be welcomed, cherished, and preserved—"United in Diversity."

We might draw already one tentative constitutional conclusion for Europe: it would appear from a survey of the European constitutional landscape that in and of itself a reference to religion, God, or Christianity in the preamble of its Constitution would not, as such, violate a European commitment to religious freedom and freedom from religion. This does not make the case for such inclusion; there might be many good reasons why such a reference should not be made, but to judge from the empirical evidence, constitutional propriety should not be considered among these good reasons.

We cannot, however, leave things at the empirical level only. Some conceptual reflection is necessary too. The case for constitutional silence on matters of religion is often argued on the ground of public neutrality. In its simplest form, the argument is that the state (and, hence, the European Union too) should not "take sides" either in the cleavage between religious and secular components of society or in demonstrating a preference for a specific religious denomination, especially in societies where other denominations exist.

This argument is not without huge difficulties.

To begin with, there is the naïve belief that for the state to be assiduously secular is to practice religious neutrality. That is false on two counts: First, there is no neutral position in a binary option. For the state to abstain from any religious symbolism is no more neutral than for the state to espouse some forms of religious symbolism. What is important is to guarantee freedom of religion and freedom from religious coercion. But the religious identity of, say, large segments of the population and the religious dimension of the culture are objective data. To deny them has nothing to do with neutrality. It is simply the privileging in the symbolism of the state of one worldview over another—all the while masquerading as neutrality.

Second, there is the delicate matter of popular preference. In our constitutional democracies, we balance democratic majoritarianism with certain constitutional guarantees to contain what has been called the tyranny of the majority. That is precisely the purpose of the religious freedom principle we find in our shared constitutional traditions: it places the right to religious freedom and the right to freedom from religion beyond the whims of any majority. But it is not an essential or integral part of those freedoms that the state, or the majority in the state, should be prevented from giving expression to the cultural facets of the national identity in the constitution. Giving such expression would seem to me to be a permissible expression of democratic preference. A state like France may legitimately wish to give expression in its democratic constitutional choice to a strict *laïque* ethos. Some might even find something to admire in a state with a Christian majority practicing such a form of restraint. But other states like Denmark, Ireland, or Germany may feel that giving expression at the constitutional level to religious expression is their way to assert their identities. Some might feel that it is even more admirable to profess at the iconographic level a strong religious identity while at the very same time guaranteeing full religious liberty to others who do not share the same religious worldview. There would, in my view, be something disturbingly antidemocratic in denying a large majority the ability to give iconographic expression to their identity (including their religious identity), as long as the constitutional principles of equality and freedom were preserved.

Of course, here too there can be delicate borderline cases, notably where a society is closely divided. Should, say, a bare Protestant majority in a country split between Catholics and Protestants (like Germany) be allowed to impose its iconography in the constitutional documents? Similarly what should one do in a polity divided more or less equally between religious and secular populations? There are two possible answers to these borderline cases. The first lies with the constitutional process—which typically requires supermajorities. The second lies with good sense: the ability in multicultural society to give iconographic expression to that very multiculturalism by acknowledging both.

We have already seen one example from Spain. Another striking example may be found in the preamble to the new Polish constitution:

> Having regard for the existence and future of our Homeland, Which recovered, in 1989, the possibility of a sovereign and democratic determination of its fate, We, the Polish Nation—all citizens of the Republic, Both those who believe in God as the source of truth, justice, good and beauty, As well as those not sharing such faith but respecting those universal values as arising from other sources, Equal in rights and obligations towards the common good—Poland. . . .

VII

And Europe as a whole? The matter seems to me somewhat simpler than the harsh debate would suggest. We have already seen that while sharing the constitutional paradigm of religious freedom, the member states and their peoples display a remarkable diversity in their understanding of the appropriateness of religious iconographic expression in the constitution. It would seem to be wrong that at the European level the constitutional position as an expression of the cultural identity of one member state would be made to prevail over all others. That is a Jacobin view of unity, totally at odds with the motto of "United in Diversity."

Europe is, of course, constitutionally committed to the principles of religious freedom. As an empirical matter, it is simply laughable not to recognize Christianity as being a hugely important element in defining what we mean by European identity—for good and for bad. In art and in literature, in music and in sculpture, even in the political culture, Christianity has been a leitmotif—an inspiration as well as an object of rebellion. *Laïcité* itself has no meaning except in opposition to religiosity, which in Europe means Christianity. There is no normativeness in affirming this empirical fact. There is only normativeness in denying it. At the same time, it is also clear that there is a very strong secular component which would feel perhaps offended if the Christian heritage were made to be the exclusive constitutional element. In this respect, Europe is much less homogeneous than, say, Ireland. Any solution should thus, as in the Polish constitution, find an elegant way to express the constitutional pluralism of Europe.

The particular formulation becomes thus a matter of democratic constitutional preference to be expressed in the process of constitution-making. What is wrong, in my view, is to skew that process of preference determination and pluralist compromise by the bogus argument that a reference to Christianity is in some ways constitutionally inappropriate. It is not. The reference to God in the German and Polish constitutions, or to the Trinity in the Irish or to Christ in the Greek or to the Catholic Church in the Spanish constitutions is every bit as European as the absence of such reference in other constitutions.

Which brings us back to the issue of Christophobia.

The point of departure here should be the convention which prepared the Charter on Fundamental Human Rights. The even-

tual compromise proposal was to include a reference to the religious heritage of Europe. Even this rather anodyne formulation
was rejected as unacceptable. There really could be no serious
constitutional grounds for such a rejection: the proof came a cou-
ple of years later when the convention preparing the draft constitution was willing to accept such a reference. By contrasting,
thus, the relative weakness of the constitutional reasoning with
the ferocity of the opposition to any explicit reference to God (as
we find, for example, in the German and Polish constitutions)
or to Christianity (as we find, for example, in the Greek, Irish,
and Danish constitutions, and of course, in the British unwritten
constitution), one is pushed to look for additional motives by way
of explaining the attitudes which eventually prevailed within the
conventions.

There is, I believe, a mixture of such motives operating at different levels of intensity in different segments of society, notably
among opinion-shaping elites.

1) Europe has had its dark moments, and European integration was constructed in the wake of its darkest moment of all.
The Holocaust, as an emblem of racial, ethnic, and religious
intolerance, will at least for some time yet cast its shadow on
European public sensibilities. A Christian Europe? What of our
Jewish citizens—those who survived our murderous hubris, our
indifference, or our cowardice? What of our Muslim citizens?
And the Roma? And all other non-Christian Europeans? Are
they not part of Europe? This is a very different argument in
the constitutional debates about church and state. The fault line
here, the cleavage, is not between the religious and the secular.
It is between the dominant culture and its minorities, between
Christians and non-Christians. Indeed, among those opposed
to a Christian allusion in the Constitution, one can find many
committed practicing Christians who believe, nonetheless, that
it would be inappropriate, not necessarily in the juridical constitutional sense, but as a matter of public decency. In the same
way that Europe in its external relations is meant to lay to rest its

colonial heritage, so it should in its internal relations lay to rest such separatism.

2) Coupled with this, and specific to the communities of believers, is no small measure of Christian guilt. Part of that guilt, too, is Holocaust-related. After Hochhuth's tendentious 1963 *Der Stellvertreter*, an open season on the Vatican and the Catholic Church became à la mode, slanderously distorting a record, which, while far from unblemished, was justly and gratefully acknowledged by survivors and victims in the immediate postwar period. Still, there is much in the conduct of both Protestant and Catholic clergy during the war which, in some manner to their credit, deeply discomfits Christians today and restrains any attempt at "pushiness" when it comes to other religious minorities.

3) Christian guilt is not just Holocaust-related. Given our new, more tolerant sensibilities toward others, there is much in the history of the West that is found today distasteful and embarrassing. There is an entire generation of opinion-shapers, now in their fifties and sixties, in the media, in letters, in politics, and in the generation of politicians now in power whose "rebellion" in their formative years was against the classical "West," against the excesses, real and presumed, of capitalism and imperialism and other "isms." There is a conflation, not entirely spurious, between the notion of Western culture and Christianity. To some, more solidly on the Left, the Church and Christianity itself are conceived as an integral part of that world and a veritable object of hostility. To others, the Church and Christianity are at least associated with that worldview, and though not the object of hostility, they are in some ways the object of embarrassment and in any event a dampener on any form of militantism.

4) Then there is, of course, politics—the vulgar, red-blooded, and instinctive repugnance between the Left and Right. In this arena, it is not about constitutional sensibility or constitutional propriety; it is the usual contestations whereby historically, at least in some of the key member states, when Christianity asserted itself

in the public space, it somehow fell on the Right. The most interesting fault line in this context is between those polities accustomed to consociational arrangements and those accustomed to
the confrontational dynamics of winner-takes-all.

5) More interesting in the psychology and sociology of Christophobia is the attitude toward the Church among the committed, less committed, and noncommitted in relation to current
Church teaching. Consider the following paradox: In an age of
celebrity, where the likes of Madonna (who some think can sing)
or Travolta (who some think can act) can fill stadia or parks with
hundreds of thousands of spectators in a manner which no politi-
cian could even dream of, the late pope John Paul II was on an
altogether different level. He drew millions, literally. And it was
not entertainment which was on display. Yet his Christian teachings were often the source of considerable hostility. The live wire
is sexuality and gender politics. The issues are well known: abortion, ordination of women, homosexuality, contraception (in the
age of AIDS), and so forth. In the eyes of some of the committed, the current teachings represent a "betrayal" of Vatican II.
The feelings can be quite intense. Among the less committed, it
is often presented (with little credibility in my eyes) as the reason for a lack of commitment. And among the noncommitted,
it becomes an easy target for hostility and even outrage at what
appears to be a reactionary, right-wing social force. I wish not to
enter into the merits of these arguments but simply to register the
phenomenon as an appreciable facet of current European attitudes toward the Church.

6) Finally, there is the personal. One cannot but notice across
Europe and across Christian denominational lines a certain gen-
erational gap: against a general landscape of weak religious practice and emptying churches, the group that most bucks this trend
is the young. The generation of most influential opinion-mak-
ers—those in their fifties and sixties—has not been caught up by
the renewed religious commitment. Indeed, part of Christophobia, confirmed to me in many conversations, is the heritage of the

personal religious experiences of this generation when growing up. This does not have to do directly with ideology. The Church of the 1950s and 1960s was, in the personal experience of many, very clerical, very establishment, very "authority." It was like school, like parents, reflecting a noninternalized set of duties with persistent memories of confessed *atti impuri*. One could not wait to get away from it. I think this experience is generalizable, with, of course, exceptions aplenty. One consequence of this is a certain carry-over of resentment and distaste. But there is a far deeper consequence: a loss of interest. I have heard again and again from my lapsed Catholic friends: "Let me tell you about the Church" or "I know all about Christianity"—but what they knew were the crumbs of childhood, the distasteful memories, the remnants from confirmation and the catechism. In fact, they often knew very little, and nothing at all of the past thirty-five or so years in the life of the Church. Significantly, keeping up with church teachings did not seem important for one's sense of being educated. One would read (or had to read at least the book review of) the latest Derrida, or Fukuyama, or Eco; one did not have to read the latest encyclical of the pope. A Christian Europe? Why? Are "they" not against contraception? Is that not what it is about?

VIII

Paradoxically, the refusal of the constitution to have a direct allusion to Christianity may in time be considered a blessing to those most keenly interested in wanting to see such a reference in the constitution. The internal walls of the European Christian Ghetto may be best illustrated if we engage in a mental exercise which imagines the opposite outcome to that which in fact occurred.

Let us first imagine that the original request for an allusion to the Christian heritage of Europe in the preamble of the charter and/or the draft constitution had been accepted. It is not unimaginable. After all, the convention's democratic self-understanding was one of its hallmarks and the request was, if not supported by, at least consistent with the wishes of a large number of Europeans.

Let us imagine further the content of such a reference. In the actual preamble to the constitution we find now the following phrase: "Drawing inspiration from the cultural, religious and humanist inheritance of Europe, the values of which, still present in its heritage, have embedded within the life of society the central role of the human person and his or her inviolable and inalienable rights, and respect for law. . . ."

Along the way a more direct allusion was also given consideration. Instead of the "cultural, religious and humanist inheritance," the reference would have been to the "Hellenic, Christian, and Humanist inheritance."

We cannot but take note of the rather pathetic nature of it all: the great engagement between the world of Christianity and European integration reduced to a word tucked between the Hellenic and the Humanist?

Indeed, in the long run, it would probably have been a brilliant Machiavellian move by those forces most opposed to any entanglement of state and church to have accepted such an allusion to the Christian tradition with the least fuss possible. It would have made some Christians happy, left most others indifferent, and the matter would have ended there. This is not inconsistent with what I have written above. The symbolic and social resonances of the rejection are far more significant than would have been a matter-of-fact acceptance by the convention.

The eventual compromise, an allusion to the religious heritage of Europe, is ironic if not comic. The irony rests with the presentation of an anthropocentric (secular) worldview as being inspired by, inter alia, the religious inheritance of Europe. If there is to be a reference to religion at all, it should respect the premises of the monotheistic Judeo-Christian tradition, in which the central role of the human person is located within a theocentric worldview and in which the rights of the person are transcendentally derived. This does not take much: consider the pithy and elegant way this is resolved in the preamble to the German constitution, pluralist and respectful of both the secular and religious, the opening phrase of which reads: "Conscious of their responsibility before God and man"—after which come the same commitments, inviolable, inalienable, and unmodifiable, to the rights of the human person and respect for the law. There can, of course, be many other ways.

Be that as it may, European Christians and Christians in Europe share in large measure responsibility for this state of affairs, both for the ease with which the request (including a request from the Holy See) to include a reference to Christianity in the preamble was rejected by the Convention and by the governments of the member states and, more importantly, for the trivialization of the entire European Christian discourse. An important part of the reason for which a reference to the Christian heritage of Europe could be dismissed with such ease is the fact that the relevance of that Christian heritage is simply not part of the intellectual patrimony of European integration. It has not been discussed, debated, contested, or defended, and most importantly, it has not been shown to be relevant, not simply as an iconographic symbol, not simply to those whose worldview is Christian, but to all, religious and secular, concerned with a deep and meaningful Europe. With few exceptions, the relevance of Christianity to the project of European integration and to the self-understanding of Europe is not clear even to Christians themselves. There is a huge literature, professional and essayistic, on the process of European integration. There are contributions to this debate from the literati and glitterati as well as us, humdrum academics, who make a living from writing. Politicians all vie to have a "Europe speech": remember Margaret Thatcher's famous anti-Europe Bruges speech? Or Joseph (Joschka) Fischer's (federal Europe) Berlin speech? But you will have to look hard to find in this vast literature works with a serious engagement between Christian thinking and European integration. We should not be misled by the "subsidiarity industry." The name was borrowed from Catholic social theory, a fact which is stated in an endless variety of ways. But for the most part, the similarities end there. For what is an important and profound principle of social responsibility has been converted to an important but vastly less profound constitutional principle of power allocation, diminished by its patent failure, to date, to deliver the objectives for which it was introduced. It thus stands today as a rhetorical constitutional palliative and exemplar of the worst of Eurospeak.

How does one explain this silence—a silence all the more surprising given that a large number of the literati and glitterati, politicians and academics, writing in the field of European integration are professing Christians?

I want to offer three possible explanations.

The first is simple enough: many have internalized the spurious constitutional logic outlined above which informs the notions of strict separation between state and church as practiced in France and, to a somewhat lesser extent, in Italy. The silence becomes thus a self-imposed silence whereby people in fact believe that it would be inappropriate for the European construct to have any reference, even preambular, even of a symbolic, identity-expressing character in the Constitution. It is not an altogether surprising internalization since it is part of the orthodoxy, indeed, of the doxy that informs our faculties and public law departments and which spills over into our public life.

The second reason, if I am correct, is more insidious. There is an internalization of a different kind. In some of our European member states, a distinction is drawn in academic life between universities and free universities. There is, thus, the University of Brussels and the Free University of Brussels. The word "Free" is, of course, a code for non-Christian or non-Catholic. In some jurisdictions, professors who join a faculty in such a free university are made to sign a document undertaking to be "free" thinkers. The implication is that to write from a religious perspective, or, indeed, to be a practicing Christian, might compromise the academic integrity of one's work. The effect in many cases can be paradoxical: religiously committed scholars and thinkers, even those working in Catholic universities—in some cases especially those working in Catholic universities—will bend over backwards to demonstrate their "free thinking" bona fides by obliterating any religious reflection, insight, or sensibility from their "professional" intellectual endeavors. Sometimes, even in their own eyes, transgressing that line is considered a failing—in others and in themselves. For many committed Christians, Church and church are put aside on Monday.

Finally, here, too, there is often ignorance or compartmentalization. Religious practice is conceived of as an exclusively spiritual experience, and the rich intellectual strata attendant on Christian teaching is either left unexplored or set aside.

IX

The failure to respect the identity reflected in the constitutions of member states representing half of Europe's population was, I have argued, a betrayal of Europe's very own self-proclaimed ideas and ideals of pluralism and tolerance. The fact that the proposed constitution eventually failed is neither here nor there if it does not occasion some serious constitutional soul-searching on this issue. Worse, the mechanical and (in my view) shallow and insubstantial reasons associated with that failure were an expression of an attitude—Christophobia—which cannot be ignored. But most worrying of all, perhaps, was the failure of the Christian community itself. Paradoxically, Europe's constitutional reality in most member states is open to the public expression of religious Christian commitment in a manner unthinkable in the current circumstance in the United States. If the European public square(s) are naked, it is because too many Christians have elected to disrobe from their glorious spiritual and cultural heritage as they enter therein.

4

Religion in a Liberal Democracy: Foundation or Threat?

Michael Pakaluk

Lessons from Europe

On October 29 of 2004 the Treaty Establishing a Constitution for Europe was signed by European Union member states after a heated discussion over whether the preamble would include mention of the Christian roots of Europe. This dispute came to be known as that of the *invocatio Dei*. But this was something of a misnomer, since there was never any question that the European Constitution would imitate, say, the constitution of Ireland, which begins: "In the Name of the Most Holy Trinity, from Whom is all authority and to Whom, as our final end, all actions both of men and States must be referred. . . ." Rather, what was at issue was simply whether the constitution would acknowledge the evident historical fact of the importance of Christianity in the formation of Europe.

Not that the history of Europe or the roots of European culture had to be mentioned at all. A constitution, strictly, doesn't even need a preamble. But given that it *was* to have a preamble, and given that, as in the so-called Giscard draft, the preamble referred to such things as "the values underlying humanism:

equality of persons, freedom, respect for reason," and also the "cultural, religious and humanist inheritance of Europe," then, in this context, not to refer to Christianity seemed a deliberate exclusion and perverse.

J. H. H. Weiler, a distinguished scholar of international law at NYU and director of the Jean Monnet Center there—himself an Orthodox Jew—in a controversial book called *Un Europa Cristiana* went so far as to argue that the exclusion of Christianity from the preamble was "unconstitutional." The purpose of a preamble, he argued, is for a people to conceptualize its own identity. If that articulation is false or is a purposeful misrepresentation, then the preamble fails on its own terms, precisely as a constitutional act. The European Constitution's preamble could not, constitutionally, intend to enumerate sources of European civilization while omitting mention of Christianity, the principal source.

Giscard d'Estaing, President of the Convention on the Future of Europe (2002–3) and the principal author of the draft constitution, objected, along with others, that to mention Christianity would be to violate "state neutrality" regarding religion. To this, Weiler retorted, What does "state neutrality" mean in this context? If, for instance, it means that the government should not coerce religious observance ("freedom from religion"), and that it should allow the free practice and expression of religion ("freedom of religion"), then clearly that sort of neutrality was consistent even with an established religion, as in England or Denmark, and therefore, a fortiori, with the mere mention of the historical importance of Christianity.

But then it was objected that to mention Christianity would be to exclude members of other religions or persons of no religious belief at all. For instance, the constitution of France, an important member of the new European Union, identifies France as "*une République indivisible, laïque, démocratique et sociale.*" How then could France, with its constitution that is *laïque*, commit itself to a union which was *not laïque*? But, as Weiler urged in reply, Why should France's "laïcism" be the default position here? Since half the people of Europe live in states the constitutions of which make explicit reference to God, why should not *that* approach win the day?

Yet it might be urged that neutrality means that the state adopts no position one way or another regarding any religion or any matter of religion: for Christianity to be mentioned in the preamble, then, would be for the state to adopt a position. Weiler pointed out that that sort of neutrality was, logically, an impossibility. "The preamble has a binary choice," he argued, "yes to God, no to God. Why is excluding a reference to God any more *neutral* than including God? It is the favoring of one worldview, secularism, over another worldview, religiosity, but masquerading as neutrality." Weiler then offered this diagnosis: "The refusal to make a reference to God is based on a false argument that conflates *secularism* with neutrality or impartiality."

We should note here that Weiler is using the word secular, as is common, to mean "nonreligious." It has been pointed out by Iain Benson in an important article that secular means, in its proper sense, *oriented toward this world*, and in this sense religious principles and people acting on religious principles may be secular.[1] Hence secularism in the correct sense does not exclude religion. (Let us from this point use the expressions "narrow" or "improper" secularism to mean a secularism which excludes religion and "broad" or "proper" secularism to mean a secularity which is consistent with religion.) What Weiler should have said, then, more precisely is that "[t]he refusal to make a reference to God is based on a false argument that defines secularism, wrongly, as the absence or marginalization of religion, and that presumes that that sort of secularism is neutral, when it is not." This improper secularism is not neutral, not merely because it necessarily adopts some definite positions rather than others ("no to God" in the preamble, in this case) but also because inevitably people are committed to it because of philosophical or metaphysical views, of which they are perhaps themselves unconscious, which play the same functional role in their lives as a religion.

If neutrality in the sense of "not taking a position" is impossible, then what should the preamble have looked like? "In its substantive provisions," Weiler summed up his case,

> the European Constitution reflects the homogeneity of the European constitutional tradition. It is fully committed to the notions of freedom of religion and freedom from religion, as it should be. But when it comes to the preamble, the EU Constitution should reflect European heterogeneity. It should reflect the European commitment to the noble heritage of the French Revolution, as reflected in, say, the French constitution, but it should reflect in equal measure the symbolism of those constitutions that include an *invocatio Dei*.

And he cited the Polish constitution as good example of this, which begins, "We, the Polish Nation—all citizens of the Republic, both those who believe in God as the source of truth, justice, good and beauty, as well as those not sharing such faith but respecting those universal values as arising from other sources, equal in rights and in obligations towards the common good. . . ."

Weiler, and others such as John Paul II, as we all know, lost the argument, and the final version of the European Constitution contains no reference to God or Christianity. This was lamentable, according to Weiler, because Europe failed miserably when it had a chance to forge a constitutional alternative to the French approach. That approach presumes, as Weiler put it, "that religion and democracy are inimical to each other: to adopt democracy means to banish God and religion from the public sphere and make it strictly a private affair." But Europe can hardly expect to be successful in spreading democracy throughout the world, Weiler pointed out, if it sends the message that the price of democracy is a system of government hostile to one's deeply held religious beliefs and practices.

Time will tell whether these and other worries of Weiler and John Paul II were correct. Yet the first signs are not encouraging. I have in mind the case of Rocco Buttiglione, apparently the first victim of a supposed spirit of "neutrality" which ends up being aggressively hostile to believing Christians.

Buttiglione, an accomplished philosopher and intellectual biographer of John Paul II, is an intellectual of the first rank, a remarkably learned and cultured man who has taught in universities across Europe and is the recipient of many honors. Mid-career he began to devote himself to public service, serving in Italy first as a member of the Chamber of Deputies of the Italian parliament and then as minister of European Union policies under Prime Minister Silvio Berlusconi. In August 2004, the president of the European Commission, José Manuel Barroso, put Buttiglione forward as one of a group of twenty-five commissioners-designate of the Directorate-General for Justice, Freedom, and Security of the European Commission.

At his confirmation hearing, Buttiglione was asked whether he regarded homosexual acts as a "sin." He did not answer directly, but only conditionally: "I may think it a sin," he said, "but in politics we may not speak of sin. We should speak of nondiscrimination, and I am solidly opposed to discrimination against homosexuals or any type of discrimination." Buttiglione also remarked, in response to another question, that he regarded a family as consisting of a man, a woman, and their biological offspring, and that the purpose of the family was that a woman could have children under the protection of the man.

These remarks led to an uproar based on media misreporting ("Being Gay Is a Sin, Says Commissioner") and a smear campaign by his political opponents. The politicians fell in line. "I would not want," remarked Josep Borell, the parliament president, "as a Spanish citizen, to have a minister of justice who thinks that homosexuality is a sin and that a woman should stay at home to have children under the protection of her husband. . . . These are shocking attitudes. That is the least that one can say. . . . It does not seem to me that in this day and age we can have people in charge of justice—especially justice—who think like that." "When I listened to him," said Bernard Poignant, president of the French socialists at the European Parliament, "I told myself that John Paul II had succeeded in sending a commissioner to Brussels!"

Buttiglione reflected later that "it was not enough" that he had said that "sin" wasn't a political category. "They wanted me to say that I see nothing objectionable about homosexuality. This I cannot do because it is not what I think." Buttiglione then said that he accepted what the *Catechism of the Catholic Church* taught, that there is a distinction between an objective disorder and a person's subjective responsibility, and that there may be "sin" if there is subjective responsibility. "I was not allowed to say that and for this reason I was deemed not worthy to be a European commissioner." As to his remarks on the family, he said, "I think that the problem of today is that a woman has the right to a professional career but she also has the right to be a mother. And we as men should not consider as second-class citizens women who freely chose not to have a career in order to consecrate themselves to the education of their children."

The Civil Liberties Committee of the European Parliament, which had to vote for or against the panel of twenty-five commissioners proposed by Barosso, voted to reject all twenty-five rather than confirm Buttiglione. Of course, no one was suggesting that all twenty-five commissioners shared Buttiglione's view—just one, and he proved to be one too many. Recognizing the political reality, Buttiglione withdrew himself from consideration (prompting other news reports along the lines of "EU Commissioner Regrets Slurs on Gays"). The lesson that many onlookers drew is that anyone who believes the teaching of the Catholic Church is disqualified to serve in the government of Europe. The supposedly neutral and inclusive secularism which was to be enshrined in the European Constitution, it seemed, excluded all Catholics, all Orthodox Jews, many Protestants, and most Muslims.

Of course one might wonder whether, really, any deep question of the compatibility of religion and democracy was raised by the Buttiglione controversy. It seems there are certain practices involving sex that some people want not simply to do without interference, but rather to do while claiming a "right" to do so—namely, sex at will outside marriage, abortion, and homosexual acts. Those matters, in recent U.S. Supreme Court jurisprudence, are assigned to the "right to privacy." Contrariwise, many religious persons hold not simply that these practices are bad and that there is no right to engage in them, but also that it is in the objective nature of things that they are bad. It is this particular claim about their objective nature—not "religion" generally—that looks like the imposition of a restriction and therefore a threat to "liberty." Religious people make a claim about how the world is for everyone. (That is why the fact that Buttiglione even *entertained* the application of the word *sin* was so detestable.) For religious persons in these matters, their beliefs function not as the sui generis source for their judgments, but rather to support judgments that they might hold even if they were not religious. A Catholic (for instance) thinks, or should think, that abortion is patently a violation of human rights—and his Catholic faith simply supports him in thinking this. A Christian might very well regard it as obvious and a matter of common humanity that there is something untoward and self-destructive about homosexual acts, and his Christian belief would work to reinforce this. It is common, of course, for someone to hold that abortion or homosexual acts are wrong before he converts to Christianity (as in my own case). Does he become disqualified from holding those views as a citizen, almost magically, because of his conversion?

It is important to stress this point, because, if Buttiglione's views were put forward in the spirit, say, of Jewish kosher law, no one would be particularly offended by them. It's precisely because his views were *secular*, in Iain Benson's sense, that they caused offense. The vehemence with which such views are greeted confirms that these views do succeed in making a claim on people generally.

These reflections invite three questions.

First, if Christian claims about morality and society are *secular* in the sense just explained, then one might wonder whether generally it is prudent for a Christian to present them as a matter of "his or her religious beliefs." Since this can serve as an excuse for his not trying to give persuasive reasons, it may invite or provoke others to dismiss one's position as one bias among others. Buttiglione said later, "I was rejected for . . . expressing my Catholic beliefs on sexuality and marriage at the hearing" and "I had the right to express my Catholic principles." Should he perhaps have left Catholicism out of it and said, simply, "I was rejected for expressing my arguments on sexuality and marriage" and "I had a right to express historically mainstream philosophical beliefs"? If he had spoken in this way, then perhaps it would have been clearer that his opponents did not have no view or a neutral view so much as an equal, opposing philosophical view.

Second, to what extent does narrow secularism depend upon relativism? Buttiglione later said that his opponents adhered to what he called the "new civil religion." "This new religion affirms that it is not permitted to have strong ethical convictions, and that democracy must base itself on relativism." The new pope, Benedict XVI, apparently in agreement with this, has gained attention for warning about a "dictatorship of relativism" that threatens genuine freedom. Yet, against this, Robert George and others maintain that narrow secularism, in important respects, is not relativistic: "While one still hears subjectivism or relativism invoked at cocktail parties . . . it seems that the heyday of moral relativism is over," George writes in *The Clash of Orthodoxies*.

> Most sophisticated secularists have concluded that relativism is ultimately inconsistent with many of their own cherished moral claims. . . . If relativism is true, then it is not wrong in principle to have an abortion, but neither is it

wrong for people who happen to abhor abortion to attempt
to legislate against it."[2]

However, George quickly qualifies what he says. He goes on to
say that narrow secularism is "in significant respects" a relativist
doctrine, but that it is "no longer a thoroughgoing and self-con-
sciously relativist doctrine."[3] So then, is it relativist or not?

Third, the "culture war" that Buttiglione (along with many
others) found himself caught up in centers around two matters:
(1) sexuality and (2) the role of religion in political life. "The issues
immediately in play," George observes, "have mainly, although
not exclusively, to do with sexuality, the transmitting and taking
of human life, and the place of religion and religiously informed
judgment in public life."[4] But why just these? George has argued
that what fuels the abortion and homosexual rights movements
is a dualist and essentially Gnostic view of the human person.
(In this he follows Walker Percy's view in *Lost in the Cosmos*.)
But why should Gnosticism care particularly about fostering a
"naked public square"? Is it that hostility to religion in public
life is a consequence of the sexual agenda, that narrow secularists sense that only moral judgment as reinforced by religion will
stand firm and resist them, and so they work for the marginalization of religion? Or is it that narrow secularism presumes that
human society, justice, and right are conventional categories of
purely human construction, not founded in anything outside us,
and so it wishes to resist any suggestion that there are constraints
or limits that are imposed "from the outside," either by God or by
nature? Religious people are detestable, then, to narrow secularists, precisely because they call attention to objective constraints
on human will, in public and in private life.

The Novelty of the Question

We understand a social reality, Aristotle said, by understanding its origin. The concern that religion might be a "threat" to

democracy is relatively new in the American and Canadian contexts; it dates only to the past forty years or so, and we want to understand why it has arisen.

It is good to remind ourselves of its novelty. In 1951, William F. Buckley Jr. published his first book, a bestseller, *God and Man at Yale*, which argued the then shocking thesis that many professors at Yale actually promoted atheism. Of course it was a commonplace during World War II and the Cold War that the democracies of the world were arrayed against "godless" dictatorships and ideologies. Bertrand Russell was denied a position at a public university in New York City in the 1940s because of his atheism. And, as David Lowenthal has brilliantly shown in his book *No Liberty for License*, U.S. Supreme Court jurisprudence which presumes that religion is a threat to freedom and consequently insists on a "strict wall of separation" began in earnest only in the 1960s. This was a departure from the inspiration of the American Framers, who took the first clause of the First Amendment, the "no establishment" clause, to be subservient to the second clause, about the "free exercise" of religion. In fact, in the drafting of the First Amendment, the Framers considered but rejected the formulation "Congress shall make no law establishing a religion," since it was thought that this would leave open whether Congress had power to disestablish the various state establishments of religion. Hence they used the language "Congress shall make no law respecting an establishment of a religion."

These constitutional provisions were supported by a corresponding public culture, which affirmed what has sometimes been called a "civil religion." Just as thought can be either theoretical or practical, so American civil religion had a theoretical and a practical aspect. The theoretical aspect was its inheritance from *Deism*. The view hammered out through religious controversies in Europe following the Reformation, Deism purports to be the "religion of reason." It says that Christianity consists solely of the doctrines of the existence of one God, the immortality of the soul, and a judgment for our deeds after death. Deists called this the "religion of nature" and held that any reasonable person could come to affirm these truths using philosophical reasoning alone. They pointed out, correctly, that these beliefs were shared by many, if not most, philosophical systems in history, and that they were at the core of all denominations of Christianity.

Deism in Europe set itself against revealed religion. For instance, a prominent Deist treatise by Matthew Tyndal was called *Christianity, A Republication of the Gospel of Nature*, which maintained that there is not, nor could there be, anything additional in Christianity beyond the reasonable beliefs of Deism. But in American civil religion, the outlook of Deism functioned in something like the manner of what was traditionally called the *praeperatio Evangelii*, "the philosophical foundation for the Gospel"; that is, Deism served as a common framework, held by Christians of all denominations (and also by Jews and philosophical theists), who nonetheless might differ on what additional doctrines were revealed. This "Deist minimum," as Avery Cardinal Dulles referred to it,[5] was commonly regarded as what any reasonable person would believe, and as such its characteristic doctrines were commonly appealed to in public discourse.

So much for the "theoretical" dimension of civil religion. But civil religion had a practical dimension as well, which we can refer to as "providentialism." This is the view that human reason, especially insofar as it is deliberative and manifests itself in skilled statecraft, is a participation in a higher reason, the providential reason of God. Providentialism holds that when we human beings reason correctly about basic matters of policy and right, we advance God's purposes, in ways we may not fully comprehend because of unforeseen consequences. Moreover, in deliberating correctly, we win for ourselves and for our descendents the blessings of prosperity. This "providentialism" is invoked constantly by American presidents and politicians. It finds expression in the noticeable confidence in *progress* that Americans have. It is evident, too, in its misuse, as in the (distorted) doctrine of "manifest destiny." But providentialism, as an aspect of civil religion, perhaps finds its high point of expression in Abraham Lincoln, not simply in his Thanksgiving Proclamation, but also in his brooding reflections, as in the Second Inaugural Address, about how God's justice was satisfied and God's purposes advanced through the sufferings of the American Civil War:

> If God wills that [the war] continue, until all the wealth piled up by the bond-man's two hundred and fifty years of unrequited toil shall be sunk, and until every drop of blood drawn with the lash, shall be paid by another drawn with the sword, as was said three thousand years ago, so still it must be said, "the judgments of the Lord, are true and righteous altogether."

So "civil religion," consisting of the "Deist minimum" together with "providentialism," was a stable, workable framework that, as we said, could win the allegiance of nearly all religions and the respect, if not the allegiance, of those who affirmed no religion at all. It had that stability because (despite what John Rawls refers to as the "burdens of judgment"—that is, the tendency of the human mind to be tentative about the most fundamental questions) this framework was easy to believe in, especially to those who were instructed in "classical civilization" from a relatively early age and who continued to study philosophical issues related to religion in a manner proportionate to their intellectual development.

What, then, disturbed this stable framework? Why, if it proved workable, has it been jettisoned in public life, even if nearly everyone, it seems, continues privately to accept it? As I said, the American and Canadian experience is distinct from that of continental Europe with its longstanding critique of religion as an instrument for domination, or as an "opiate of the masses" (as for Marx), or as a "projection of the Father figure" (as Freud thought). Moreover, the reasons for the continental critique—a jealous concern for autonomy which looks at an appeal to God as "heteronomous"—seem not to have been important historically in North American political thought.

No major social change or revolution—and the change that took place in the 1960s is indeed a revolution in the sense that previously marginal outlooks gained dominance, and previously dominant outlooks became marginal—occurs without a confluence of distinct and accidental causes, even if it is possible to identify one cardinal cause on which other causes hinge.

I think we can distinguish both *political* and *cultural* causes of the revolution.

The political causes had the character of incremental changes that seemed good, each in its place, but which eventually had consequences that were not intended.

One such political cause is the constitutional theory of "incorporation" embraced by U.S. courts. I mentioned earlier that the Establishment Clause of the First Amendment was meant to preserve the prerogative of states to establish their own religions. That prerogative was negated when, much later, courts began to regard that clause as "incorporated" into the Fourteenth Amendment's due process clause and therefore to extend analogously to state governments, vis-à-vis their citizens. A consequence of the doctrine of incorporation is that government in general is thought to have the same relationship to individual persons as the federal government originally had toward individual states.

Another important political factor was the prestige of the civil rights movement in the 1960s, which seemed to verify the principle that local restrictions on action, or local distinctions (such as "separate but equal"), precisely because they are local and not universal, are arbitrary and irrational, and that therefore the actions of a higher authority (such as the Supreme Court), in vindicating the freedom of action of individuals against the restrictions of local authority, count always as an increase in freedom.

The effect of both of these changes was to undermine the notion of "subsidiarity" and to foster a reconception of society (as

Robert Nisbet has pointed out) as a monolithic "state" set over and against a collection of atomized individuals.[6] What falls by the wayside are "mediating institutions" with real authority, and even the notion of the family as the basic cell of society, in relation to which political society, although natural and inevitable, is derivative. Political society now looks like the primary society to which someone belongs. Religious obligations are no longer conceived of as original obligations which a person has prior to any obligations he may owe to the state. The upshot is that religion looks like the project of individuals, and religious allegiance gets assimilated to other incidental preferences (what Stephen Carter calls the "culture of disbelief").

These are political changes with their unintended consequences. They could not have had those consequences, however, unless there were corresponding cultural changes. The most important of these, in my view, was the loss of clarity, coherence, and historical faith among mainline Protestant denominations, precisely when mainline Protestantism was functioning effectively as an established religion in the United States. This was a consequence of "theological liberalism," which, under the influence of American pragmatism, converted mainline Protestant denominations into advocates of a largely secularized "social gospel."

The chief way in which this loss of coherence operated on the culture was through the secularization of prominent universities in the twentieth century—exactly what Buckley drew attention to. This secularization took place within a span of about fifty years. George Marsden, for instance, has an article "God and Man at Yale, 1880," in which he describes how Noah Porter, the president at Yale, spoke at the founding of Wellesley College, the founding documents of which declared, "The Institution will be Christian in its influence, discipline, and course of instruction."[7] In Porter's speech, he argued that this was correct, that universities could not be neutral. They had to be either for Christianity or implicitly against it: "Ethics, politics, and social science suppose a decisive position to be taken one side or the other in respect to both theism and Christianity," Porter said. "[E]ven elementary treatises on these subjects teach a positive faith or a positive a denial." In universities and colleges, young persons are introduced to a framework that they understand to be "what reasonable people think" and that they adopt for life. If a university claims to teach all knowledge, but does not teach theology, or anything definite about religious matters, then a presupposition, built into its very structure, is that there is no theological knowledge. If a university claims to debate and consider all questions, but discussions of religious matters are put to the side, then it adopts, as a working presupposition, that there can be no reasonable discourse on these matters. It would be natural for someone educated in this way to conclude implicitly that, if political discourse is supposed to be reasonable, yet reasonability does not include religion, then religion is not supposed to be included in political discourse. Young people are perceptive and smart. They will sense and assimilate these presuppositions.

The secularization of the universities in the mid-twentieth century, then, explains the widespread view in the late twentieth century that religion is an irrational bias with no special claim to be expressed in the public realm, and which even, perhaps, is something to be avoided, because it is dogmatic and absolutist, and therefore tends to fanaticism. (This last touch reflects the distinctive influence of American pragmatism and fallibilism.)

Now combine this cultural change with the sexual revolution of the 1960s, and one finds exactly the combination of issues that Robert George drew attention to. As for the sexual revolution, it seems to have been precipitated in large part through the widespread acceptance of the notion, seemingly fostered by artificial birth control, that sexual satisfaction may licitly be detached from considerations of childbearing and long-term commitment. When sexual satisfaction is thus detached, then human action becomes guided by an aggressive and expansionist principle of sexual desire or "concupiscence" (to use an old-fashioned word), which shapes public life. This principle is *expansionist* because, by the very nature of the desire, it has to make ever greater demands to find satisfaction; and it is *aggressive* because it takes resistance to its demands at the progressive boundary to be resistance to the whole.

Does Rawls Avoid the Pitfalls?

As we have seen, narrow, nonreligious secularism is relativistic but thinks that it is not; it thinks it does not presuppose any substantive view, and yet it does. I want to conclude by considering briefly whether John Rawls, especially in his notion of "public reason," succeeded in putting forward a political outlook that avoids these traps. I should say at the outset that I regard Rawls's motives as unimpeachable. Without question, he intended to construct a framework for social cooperation that was neutral and also accommodating of diverse philosophical and religious views. He strove mightily to do so. Yet at the same time, I believe that he failed and, since his followers typically think that he has succeeded, the net effect of his philosophy has been to confirm secularists in their false consciousness so that they continue to impose policies through the courts, which they take to be neutral, when in fact the policies presuppose controversial and even unsustainable views; moreover, Rawlsians regard these policies as compromises which others should reasonably accept, dismissing complaints to the contrary as sectarian and biased.

The basics of Rawls's view are easy to state, and, in a sense, the basic ideas are all that concern us, since these are what even more advanced students will typically carry with them into practical life.[8] In essence, Rawls is concerned with two ideas: political society, as a distinct form of association; and civic friendship, as a distinct form of resolving disagreements. Rawls's philosophy is largely an attempt to get clear about these two things. I say "to get clear about" them because Rawls thinks that we citizens of modern, liberal democracies already have a good practical grasp of what they are since we are engaged in these things. In the way that a grammarian might aim to state rules that express how people already speak—and in stating those rules he enunciates also a standard or ideal of grammaticality—so Rawls aims to make explicit and idealize what, he thinks, we are already doing.

This, by the way, is the reason Rawls has been called, not without reason, a historicist and a pragmatist. He is a historicist because he takes free political society as a given: he thinks that his reflections would have little force in, say, the Mongolia of Ghengis Khan or the Scottish highlands in the late Middle Ages. He is a pragmatist insofar as he thinks that it is possible that patterns of action and practices can be free-standing, without the need for any doctrines to underwrite them.

One might think at this point that Rawls has already committed himself to some fairly hefty philosophical views, and that if this is what his "neutrality" amounts to, then it is a philosophical flop. I would agree with that assessment in the end. Yet it would be too quick to make that judgment at this point, because, as we shall see, Rawls thinks that someone can accept his notions without accepting also the way in which Rawls, in particular, justifies those notions.

Let us return to the notions of political society and civic friendship. First, political society. By political society I mean basically what Aristotle meant by *koinônia politikê*: that there is a mode of association (a *koinônia*), distinct from relationships within a family, clans, business partnerships, voluntary associations, and religious groups, and which is a "complete association," in which we relate to one another as distinct persons who are free and equal. (It is complete because it provides the "basic structure" for human life, as Rawls puts it.) Readers of Aristotle's *Politics* may remember that he complains that Plato made the mistake of treating all associations as if they were the same in kind, differing only in degree—that being a king was just the same as being a father, except the former involved more subjects.

Aristotle also objects that Plato takes the relationship between the best of friends, for whom "all things are in common," as a paradigm of the sort of unity that would prevail in an ideal state. That sort of closeness, Aristotle says, would effectively destroy the state because a state is essentially composed of diverse elements. Distinctively political association is destroyed if the state is analogized to a single organism.

Rawls's philosophical career began with his putting forward a similar objection to utilitarianism. At that time, in the 1960s, utilitarianism held sway as a theory of both personal action and public policy. As Charles Taylor has pointed out, utilitarianism was the dominant view because of its apparent rigor: it seemed to be the only "scientific" theory of ethics which employed methods similar to those of the natural sciences.[9] Rawls's objection, in effect, was that whatever the merits of utilitarianism as a theory for personal action, it failed as an account of deliberation in a liberal society, because, as he put it, utilitarianism "denies the distinctness of persons." In aggregating, for purposes of calculation, the weal and woe of distinct members of society, and particularly in allowing the weal of one person to compensate for the woe suffered by another, utilitarianism treats those persons as if they were parts of a single body.

Rawls then put forward a version of contractarianism, familiar from Hobbes, Locke, and Rousseau, using the latest developments in game theory and decision theory, so that his theory had a rigor that could compete with that of utilitarianism. This was his famous argument "from the Original Position." It goes as follows: Let us presume that liberal political society is a distinct form of association; it is a stable, complete association of distinct persons who regard one another as free and equal. The crucial question to ask, Rawls says, is "What are the fair terms of cooperation for that sort of association?" But fair terms, Rawls maintains, are terms that would be arrived at by negotiators who were fairly situated. Obviously, to be "fairly situated" is an ideal. Rawls claims we can get clear about this ideal by a thought exper-

iment, wherein we imagine people about to form a political association: they consider various terms that might govern their association and select some of these as being preferable. Rawls says
that, because unavoidably people will have diverse philosophical
and religious views, and because unavoidably people will vary in
natural gifts, in fortune, and therefore in economic success, we
should imagine that these people about to form a political society
do not know in advance what philosophical or religious views
they will hold and do not know what their economic status will
be. That is, we place them under a "Veil of Ignorance," as Rawls
calls it.

Rawls argues that no one who was fairly situated in this sense
would agree to live in a society in which the standard list of
human rights was not recognized and that no one would agree to
live in a society where disparities in wealth did not work out for
the benefit of all. These two principles, then, are the fair terms
of cooperation for political society—first, respect for the equal
rights of all, and, second, a toleration of economic disparity only
to the extent that it works out for the benefit of the least advan-
taged members of society.

I omit the details, but such is essentially Rawls's view in his
1971 classic, *A Theory of Justice*. But time marches on, and with
it the incessant dialectic of critical thought. Rawls's arguments
were immediately subjected to sustained criticism. In the decades
that followed, it began to seem that nearly everything about
the theory was controversial. Indeed, Rawls's view looked to be
just one particular philosophical view among others, as sectarian as any other view. Therefore Rawls took steps to disentangle
the principles of justice he had formulated from his particular
method of justifying them. He came to think that "fair terms of
cooperation" for a diverse and pluralistic society, by the nature of
the case, could not depend essentially on some single method of
arriving at them.

Thus Rawls in the late 1980s and 1990s developed what he
called "political liberalism," a theory of the state that, as he put

it, is "political" (that is, *pragmatist*) rather than "metaphysical."
If political theory is "political, not metaphysical," there is no
need to accept Rawls's own favored method of arriving at the
principles of justice: one man might affirm them because he is a
Thomist; another, because he is a Lockean; another, because he
finds them in the Bible; another, because he finds them in the
Tao; and so on. That is, in a pluralistic society, these principles
can and should be justified by what Rawls refers to as an "overlapping consensus." The principles are held in common, but the
means of justifying them are diverse.

Futhermore, Rawls said, when people deliberate in common
in light of these principles, as regards matters of basic justice, they
should do so simply by relying on the core notion of "political association as involving distinct persons who are free and equal." They
should not rely on any particular philosophical or metaphysical
views or expect others to be swayed by such considerations because
not everyone will share these views. Rawls refers to this sort of
deliberation as "public reason." I said earlier that there were two
basic notions of Rawls's philosophy, a conception of "political association" and of "civic friendship." "Public reason" is a conception
of civic friendliness. It presumes that, if we are associating with
one another as free and equal persons, then we won't want to use
coercion against the other. Or, rather, we would use coercion just
insofar as the other would want it to be applied to himself, if he
were reasonable. It is not unlike how one brother might never want
to force his brother to do something—except when his brother is
drunk, delirious, not in his right mind, or otherwise unreasonable.
Then he will use coercion, thinking that if and when his brother
comes to his senses, he'll see that he was simply forced (as Rousseau
puts it in his *Contract Sociale*) to do what he willed to do anyway.
Similarly, no one who had the right attitude of friendliness would
ever propose as law in political society something which the other
could not reasonably accept on his own terms.

Such is Rawls's view. He thinks that there is this freestand-
ing conception of political association already implicit in how we

act; and he thinks that we can identify it, get clear about it, and reason about basic issues of fairness in light of it without appeal to particular philosophical or religious views.

Now, there is no doubt that Rawls wants to articulate such a conception. But does he succeed in doing so? Does such a conception exist? Or, if it exists, does it alone have enough content really to be useful in resolving any controversy one way or another?

We can approach this matter by posing the following question, which is an analogue of that faced by the drafters of the European Constitution. Suppose that we gave the negotiators in Rawls's Original Position the following choice: "Do you wish to adopt Rawls's two principles of justice (that is, equal human rights and economic inequality only insofar as that works out to the benefit of all), or do you wish to adopt those two principles *plus* an *invocatio Dei*, which proclaims that God exists, that we are made in his image, and that our rights and blessings derive from God?" Which set of principles do you think the deliberators in the Original Position would choose?

A Rawlsian might say that, since the deliberators are behind the Veil of Ignorance and so do not know whether they will be theists or atheists in the society to be founded, they would choose the minimalist path and omit an *invocatio Dei*.

Yet would not this response involve precisely the same mistake that Weiler had pointed out regarding the European Constitution? We've presented a binary choice to the deliberators: yes to God or no to God. If they include the *invocatio Dei*, then this would (perhaps) be a burden to atheists, but, similarly, if they omit the *invocatio Dei*, is not this (perhaps) just as much a burden to theists? Either (1) God is invoked in a society in which some citizens think God does not exist; or (2) God is not invoked in a society in which some citizens think that God does exist (and therefore *should* be recognized). The two results seem equal; neither seems more "neutral" than the other.

Again, we might wonder what precisely the Veil of Ignorance involves. Rawls says that the negotiators should be ignorant of what philosophical and religious views they are to hold and also of the economic status they are to have. It is clear why these things should be shrouded in ignorance. But what about basic facts about the natural world and basic knowledge? Rawls says, sensibly enough, that the deliberators in the Original Position should not be ignorant of these things. The reason is that they are supposed to be ideal deliberators, and in deliberation, as economists say, "more information is better than less." Indeed, Rawls says that they will have accurate knowledge about the world. But then, do they know the following things? Do they know that God exists, that human beings are made in God's image, and that human rights and the good things we enjoy derive from God? And, if they do know this, why ever would they agree to enter into a society in which these truths were deliberately circumscribed and rendered such that no one using public standing or authority could affirm them? Presumably these truths are extremely important; to circumscribe them in that way would be irrational, if not perilous.

A Rawlsian might retort, "You *believe* that God exists; you do not *know* it." We retort (accepting the Deist's arguments), "No, we *know* this, in much the same way as we know other things—and, besides, don't you need a substantive philosophical view to defend this distinction between *believing* and *knowing* which you are invoking?"

The Rawlsian then says, "You may 'know' that God exists, yet others 'know' that God does not exist." To which we say, "Precisely. But then why should I employ that other person's view of what I know, rather than my own?"

The Rawlsian might retort, "We ascribe to the negotiators in the Original Position all *scientific* knowledge, all *true* knowledge. But theology is not a science, and that God exists is not something that people know." But then it is clear that, if *that* is how the response goes, then the Rawlsian enterprise indeed presupposes positivism and agnosticism. In sum: if God's existence and our dependence upon him is something we know, then there is no reason not to ascribe this knowledge to deliberators in the Original Position, in which case, arguably, they would not agree to principles of justice that failed to give due recognition to God, and only a corresponding, substantive philosophical view can gainsay this.

There are lots of other reasons for holding that Rawls fails to state a "neutral" view. For instance, any sound political society needs to do more than articulate "fair terms of cooperation among free and equal persons": it also needs to say which beings count as persons and therefore enjoy the protection of rights—those who are the "subjects of justice." By the nature of the case, this requires a substantive, philosophical position. Is it that all sentient beings, insofar as they are sentient, have rights (as Peter Singer thinks[10])? Or only those beings who, in addition to being sentient, can form some kind of concept of oneself (as Michael Tooley thinks[11])? Or perhaps only the Aryan race (as Hitler thought)? Or only white persons from Europe (as Stephen Douglas seemed to have thought)? Or only born or viable human beings (as the U.S. Supreme Court has determined)? One might say, in the manner of Ronald Dworkin, that "public reason" does not *deny* that unborn children have rights, it merely *fails to affirm* this. But then one might reply that it requires a substantive view to hold that public categories of personhood need not track actual categories. If a Rawlsian says, at this point, "It's only *your* view that the unborn are persons," we can say, "It's only *your* view that maybe they're not."

As regards Rawls's notion of "public reason," I've given simply a sketch of it, but it is a difficulty whether anyone *could* give anything more than such a sketch. Rawls claims that such a method of reasoning exists, without saying much about *how* it works or giving many *examples* of it. And the examples he does give are worrisome. I am familiar with three examples he offers. First, there is the famous abortion footnote (in the first edition of *Political Liberalism*), where Rawls asserted, "I believe any reasonable balance . . . will give a woman a duly qualified right to decide whether or not to end her pregnancy during the first trimester. The reason for this is that at this early stage of pregnancy the political value of the equality of women is overriding, and this right is required to give it substance and force."[12] He was roundly criticized for this and had to withdraw it. Second, he says that he regards the jurisprudence of the U.S. Supreme Court as an "exemplar of public reason," which is strange, since it is demonstrable that those opinions everywhere rely upon substantive views.[13] Third, in his "Reply to Habermas," he says that he does not regard the U.S. Constitution as an ideal expression of public reason; he claims that, among other things, the Constitution ought really to mandate "public financing for political elections," that it is not sufficiently distributivist since "it allows a widely disparate distribution of income and wealth," and that it should also mandate "health care for [the] many who are uninsured." These policies are all worth deliberating or debating, of course, but to presume, as Rawls must if he thinks they should be built into the Constitution, that policies of this sort are dictates of neutral public reason seems naïve at best.

In sum, it seems that Rawlsian "public reason" is faced with a dilemma. If it is to be a neutral framework acceptable to all, then it settles nothing. If it is given enough content so as to settle anything, then it cannot but be substantive and controversial, and there would seem to be no reason why other substantive and controversial views should not also be relied upon, such as natural law theory.

Conclusion

What should we conclude from all this? May I suggest the following tentative conclusion? When our having to make a decision about a social policy places us in, as Weiler put it, a "binary choice" situation, then, logically, in those circumstances there is no impartial or neutral ground, and any view which purports to be neutral imports surreptitiously a substantive view, and furthermore it does so unfairly, because this view is not explicitly brought to light and held up for debate. Good statecraft will often involve either keeping such "binary choice" situations from arising (because they make inevitable a kind of civil strife) or, when such situations do arise, asking what substantive view can *best*, albeit imperfectly, incorporate different points of view.

It is possible to avoid "binary choice" situations by making a distinction whereby one thing is affirmed as good (or bad) globally, but another is allowed to exist and be pursued as bad (or good) locally. A good example of this is how the American Framers dealt with the issue of slavery. As Lincoln pointed out, although the Constitution did allow for Southern states to recognize slavery, it did so conceiving of it as a local institution with only a temporary existence, which was "in course of extinction."[14] The Framers deliberately avoided even using the word "slave" in the document, in order to preserve the judgment, on behalf of the Republic as a whole, that slavery was evil. This shrewd statecraft was upset, however, by the Kansas-Nebraska act, which made it an open question whether slavery could be extended into the territories, and then again by the Supreme Court in *Dred Scott*, which discovered incorrectly in the Constitution a positive "right" to own slaves. This led to a "binary choice" situation in each new territory: slavery had to be either affirmed by everyone as good or denied by everyone as evil; there was no middle ground. And this precipitated outright civil war.

In closing let me propose, provocatively, that efforts to extend the notion of marriage to same-sex relationships similarly force "binary choice" situations. As John Finnis points out, in European and indeed in much of Anglo-American law, a fairly stable compromise position was arrived at, whereby society "globally" articulated the judgment that homosexual actions were bad, while "locally" and privately people were allowed to pursue such actions. The compromise was stable, because it involved reciprocity: the political body allows the practice in exchange for retaining the authority to call it wrong. Hence, legal recognition of same-sex marriage upsets this compromise and destroys reciprocity because it seeks to secure *both* allowance to act *and* immunity from moral criticism.

That this is so is evident, I think, in the line of judgments culminating in the Supreme Court of Canada's decision in *Chamberlain v. Surrey*.[15] The British Columbia Court of Appeals had employed the notion of subsidiarity and parental authority to preserve some kind of global/local distinction: in its view society would globally affirm the goodness of homosexual relationships, while in limited circumstances involving very young children, particular school districts would be able to act as though they regarded these as wrong.

But the Canadian Supreme Court, then, rules out any such distinction and compels a policy which the Court takes to be neutral, but which clearly is not, because the policy is implemented now in a "binary choice" situation. There are only two views, and these are exclusive: one view is that a mother, father, and their biological children is a family in a strict, central, and ideal sense, and that this arrangement is better than others; the other view is that, as the book *Asha's Mums* states, a family is any group of people who "live together and love each other," and that no such group is better than any other. Since these views are incompatible, there can be no policy that is neutral between them. And this is clear from the Court's decision. When the Court insists that "all families are to be respected" is a neutral principle, it fails to see that it has adopted the substantive view of what a family is. (In fact, it has adopted the same view as stated in *Asha's Mums*.) When the Court insists that the "interests of same-sex families should be taken into account," and books such as *Asha's Mums* should be read to kindergarteners, it fails to see that those interests cannot be taken into account without at the same time, in an equally serious way, not taking into account the strictly incompatible interests of families who hold that same-sex families are not ideal for children.

Now, if the Court were not caught in narrow secularist "false consciousness," then it might have recognized that to use only books portraying traditional marriage in kindergarten instruction does not, of itself, imply the wrongness of other arrangements, whereas to use books portraying alternative family arrangements in kindergarten instruction does, itself, imply the wrongness of the view that traditional marriage is the ideal. (Why? Because we normally do not hold up as models for kindergarteners living arrangements that we believe are harmful or destructive.) Hence, the most inclusive policy, in fact, would be that which the School Board of Surrey, B.C. had originally decided upon. And thus the Supreme Court would have let the much more prudent decision of the Appeals Court stand.

And note too that all of this can be said without any mention—prejudicial mention, I would say—of the religious beliefs of those who objected to *Asha's Mums*. And the reason for this is that their views are, after all, secular, in the proper sense of that term. Their judgment about what is in the true interests of children is very much a secular judgment, even if it is grounded in a strongly held religious view of the world.

Part Two

Religion and Pluralist Democracy

5

Telling the Truth about God and Man in a Pluralist Society: Economy or Explication?

John Finnis

The identification of human flourishing's basic aspects can be made and defended against objections and misunderstandings without appealing to any idea of divine causality, still less to any idea of a divine will about what we should and should not choose. The inquiry into human flourishing can proceed without adverting to the question of divine existence; the good of relating appropriately to a transcendent and intelligent source of everything we know of can be postulated without being affirmed—can be left, that is, as a kind of space in the account of human flourishing, to be occupied by the good we call *religion* if further inquiry shows that such a being must be judged to exist. Accordingly, when one pursues (a) the inquiry into the principles of practical understanding that direct us toward the basic aspects of human flourishing, and (b) the inquiry into the rational requirement that one remain open in all one's deliberation and choice to the directiveness of each of those first principles, and likewise (c) the inquiry into the implications of that requirement, implications we call morality, one can proceed, rather as one does in the natural sciences, without adverting to the *further question*: the question whether the fact that all these principles are true, and the fact that we have the capacity to recognize that and to shape ourselves and the world accordingly, are not facts that can be explained only as effects of a causality that, by reason of *what* its causer is, needs no further explanation. That further question could be postponed to the end, or at least to the end of my books *Natural Law and Natural Rights* and *Fundamentals of Ethics*; obviously, if its answer is positive, the implications need taking up and being given their due importance in due course.

The decision to structure my books in that way was in some respects methodologically motivated: the study of metaphysics, of the foundations of all knowing and being, properly comes last (as Aquinas and Aristotle say). But my procedure was also an exercise in what John Henry Newman, following the Alexandrian Church Fathers of the third century A.D., called *economy*: the adapting of exposition to the receptiveness, the state of mind, of one's expected audience. The idea of economy, in this or related senses, has gotten a bad name: a recent head of an Oxford college, when he was secretary of the cabinet and head of the U.K. Civil Service, was pilloried for testifying that he thought it proper in the interest of the state sometimes to be "economical with the truth." Newman himself was given occasion to write his famous *Apologia pro Vita Sua* by widely applauded accusations of dishonesty by Charles Kingsley—made because that best-selling children's author and cleric equated economy with deviousness, evasion, and deception. But from the outset of his teaching, Newman had insisted on the line separating those vices of dishonesty from a rightly discreet *stewardship of the truth* by presenting always what is true, withholding no more of the relevant truth than the ignorance or prejudices of one's hearers would prevent them from properly understanding and assessing.[1] My procedure was indeed less economical than the decision of my mentor and editor H. L. A. Hart to leave undisclosed in all his public work his own atheism and his vigorous doubt that there are any moral truths whatever. After all, Chapter 13 of my *Natural Law and Natural Rights* is right there in the hands of every reader of the book, with its argument, pursued over some pages, that the "further question" of the origin of everything we come to acknowledge can only be answered reasonably by judging that—to put the matter as shortly as it can be put—God exists, and that God's intelligent and necessarily free choice to create is that needed explanation.

Practicing a similar economy even more strenuously in my *Aquinas*, I abstracted from the great theologian's theological concerns and foundations until, again, the last chapter, where I set out a version of each of the four or five kinds of ways of posing and pressing the "further question," ways which he rightly thinks show that it is unreasonable not to judge that the universe as a whole and in every aspect is the effect of the creative action of a being that is (i) pure actuality free from every shadow of mere potentiality, (ii) a reality whose *what* it is includes *that* it is, (iii) a being with all the uncaused and necessary existence that the entire universe of contingently existing and transient realities would lack even if it happened to have existed from eternity, (iv) a being which has projected some of its own intelligent intelligibility into the universe that it has freely—from among all alternative possible universes—brought into being and actuality. "The causing, ordering, and sustaining of the universe must, therefore," I wrote in *Aquinas*, "be an intellectual act which in one and the same timeless act both projects (by practical understanding) and effects (by willing), in every detail, this world with all its causal/explanatory systems, its unimaginable galaxies, subatomic particles, and fundamental forces—a world, too, of genomes, cells, and brains; of mathematics and logic which (even without aspiring to) fit that world; of loyalty, justice, and remorse; of computers, symphonies, chess, and constitutions."[2]

In *Aquinas*, I turn from that point to try to explicate, in barest outline, how these conclusions affect the understanding of the ethical and political principles and virtues explored in the preceding eleven chapters. A part of this explication follows:

The principles of practical reasonableness are now understandable as having the force and depth of a kind of sharing in God's creative purpose and providence.[3] The good of practical reasonableness (*bonum rationis*) is now understandable as good not only intrinsically and for its own sake but also as a constituent in the good of *assimilatio* (making oneself like)[4] and *adhaesio* (uniting oneself) to the omnipotent creator's practical wisdom and choice. The truth of the practical principles is now understandable not only as the anticipation of the human fulfillment to which they direct us,[5] but also as their conformity to the most real of all realities, the divine creative mind, the mind which is nothing other than the very reality of that pure and simple *act*, God.[6]

There is a lot more to be said along these lines, but there are two points to be made here about what is going on in these and similar discussions. The first is that the whole course of reflection, heading toward the reasonable judgment that God (a) exists and is (b) relevant to understanding more adequately why our responsibilities matter, is an exercise in *public reason*. The second is that the argument's conclusion entails that neither atheism nor radical agnosticism is entitled to be treated as the "default" position in public reason, deliberation, and decisions. Those who say or assume that there is a default position and that it is secular in *those* senses[7] (atheism or agnosticism about atheism) owe us an argument that engages with and defeats the best arguments for divine causality. Only if some counterargument of this kind were successful would they be entitled to set aside the judgment of the countless many who, even when they could not articulate formal arguments for it, have been able to judge that the reality and intelligibility of this world has been brought (and is kept) from nothingness by something that utterly transcends it and whose "glory," as the Psalmist says, "is declared by the heavens."[8] The heavens are the part of this world we most easily contemplate for what it *is* without mixing in our own concerns with using or relating to it. They also arouse in us the thought that we are not in a world closed off in death and finitude, but in a reality that opens out into transcendence.

Still, public reason's deliberative, practical part does deal with matters that concern us because, unlike God, they can be brought into being, changed, or averted by our choice and action. These are the deliberations for which the principles understood in practical reason—principles of natural law, if you like—give their directions, their prescriptions. The purpose of all the earlier chapters in these books of mine was to show how moral rules and principles, not least those we use more or less uncontroversially throughout our law, are explicable by reference to the more general and first principles of intelligent thinking about what to do, taken with a sound and exact understanding of what—what kind of act—one elects to do when one has deliberatively shaped alternative proposals for action and made one's choice by adopting one of them. The common objection to this whole idea is that it fails because the principles it identifies command none of the consensus that, say, good science confidently expects and commonly gets. The objection uses the fact of pluralism as an argument for skepticism about natural law, but really (therefore) about all ethical propositions.

The objection is invalid. The truth of ethical claims is assessed not by looking to facts such as people's agreement or disagreement with them but by considering whether the claims correctly identify how the kind of action (or abstention) in an issue relates to the well-being of human persons (human flourishing), and whether they rightly evaluate that relationship. The standards of rightness and wrongness in such assessments are identified in the reflective, critically clarified practical understanding and reasoning we call ethics. Consensus around those standards is not what makes them true and is not a necessary condition of that truth in any sense save this: that under *ideal* epistemic conditions, there would be consensus on them. That there would be consensus under ideal conditions on a proposition's truth is a "mark"—not a criterion—of that proposition's truth.[9] But the conditions under which any and every moral proposition is in fact assessed are very far indeed from ideal. We have strong emotional interests in securing certain outcomes which would be blocked by any reasonable ethical standard. Our capacity to devise rationalizations for departing from reasonable ethical standards to secure those interests is very great. The tendency for language, institutions, and culture to crystallize around such plausible (albeit unreasonable) rationalizations is very strong, resulting in local (but perhaps widespread and rather lasting) subscription, tending toward consensus, on distorted standards and ethical falsehoods. The pluralism of ethical opinions about more or less specific kinds of action is precisely the kind of diversity one would expect, even though there is some impressive consensus on the more general principles.

The past forty years have provided strikingly clear examples of the way in which the descent from high-level general principles to specific moral rules and judgments is waylaid by emotions, mixed motives, and rationalization. Even in the mid-1960s, after eighty years of passionate feminist campaigning about birth control as a necessary alleviation of the difficulties and dangers faced by women in and after pregnancy, the idea that a mother has a right, moral or legal, to choose to seek the death of the child she has conceived was virtually unheard of, had no perceptible presence in the literature, and had been implicitly repudiated as unethical and unacceptable by main leaders among the feminist advocates of birth control. But then, within ten years, that idea became, as it remains, a commonplace for many (albeit without consensus about its basis or limits). Yet it remained and remains in the view of many others a simply false claim of right. To me, its acceptance seems a paradigmatic instance of the process by which moral truth becomes obscured, and a vivid illustration of the way that nonideal epistemic conditions block the attainment or retention of consensus on moral propositions. But there are plenty of other paradigmatic instances. In my book with Joseph Boyle and Germain Grisez on nuclear deterrence, we trace the historical process by which a consensus that civilians should not be intentionally selected for destruction was lost, and the moral truth considerably (though by no means wholly) obscured, under the nonideal epistemic conditions prevailing in Europe in 1941 and in the Pacific in 1945.[10]

But of course, epistemic conditions are never ideal, even in the natural sciences and mathematics, where ambitions, fears, uncriticized conventions and assumptions, and other such factors can and do distort rational inquiry and judgment. All the more so in moral reasoning. Moral reasoning always concerns premises and conclusions, principles and judgments that are liable to affect profoundly our *interests* and the passions, strong or calm, whose objects are wrapped up in those interests. And the impact of familial, local, and national conventions and prejudices is particularly formative of the elements with which we conduct our moral reasoning. (As Aristotle says, you should pray that you happened to grow up in a morally more or less sound culture, since if you did not, your ability to do ethics soundly is all but irremediably weakened.[11] He did not mean, of course, that culture or convention, even when morally sound, is the *criterion* of what is sound and unsound in ethics.)

Hence it is hard, though by no means impossible, to think soundly about moral matters, not least about the issues that concern not the forms of human good, but rather the makeup and dignity of human persons, or the proper description of human acts—issues that, though not in themselves practical, normative, "ought" questions, nonetheless directly enter into and affect moral judgments. Now if (a) consistently sound moral thought is difficult to achieve and maintain, and if (b) at the same time it is the case that the moral principles which are the criteria of moral soundness and unsoundness are, like every other intelligibility that we find rather than make, to be attributed to the wisdom and will of a divine creator—as the arguments I sketched earlier indicate they should—then (c) it is reasonable to anticipate that this supremely intelligent creator of less adequate intelligences like ours might communicate those same moral principles in a way that renders them more clearly accessible and more palpably warranted. And that anticipation is satisfactorily met, fulfilled, as one aspect of the public revelation in Jesus Christ.

So the issue at the heart of my reflections today is the status of public revelation in public reason. Revelation of God's nature and intentions for us is "public," in the focal sense, when it is offered in public preaching attested to by signs or miracles such as resurrection, otherwise inexplicable healing, fulfillment of prophecies, and so forth. But the evidentiary force of these is immeasurably enhanced by, perhaps even dependent upon, the further fact that the teaching to whose authenticity they are meant to attest, a teaching by word and deed, is itself *morally* attractive. As I once summarized Aquinas, "The revelatory power and credit-worthiness of Christ's teaching should be ascribed also to [besides miracles and other public signs] his persuasive authority and manifest personal virtue, and the inherent excellence of what he taught—something he deliberately left to be judged from the public preaching and writing of those who had witnessed his own public life and works."[12]

In other words, we bring to our hearing of the preaching and assessment of its teachers and witnesses our prior understanding of human good, an understanding that is, as I have argued, at root our natural reason. And we use that as a criterion in judging for ourselves the authenticity, the divine origin, of what is being proposed and displayed to us. Yet, in turn, the preaching, the witness, and the exemplary lives of the teachers can and do change our prior moral understanding, enhancing and correcting it. There is a reciprocity and a certain kind of epistemic interdependence of natural reason and divine public revelation, interdependence which heads toward a kind of reflective equilibrium (as Rawls might say[13]).

That reflective equilibrium is not in all respects a once-for-all achievement, but rather is to some extent developmental, both in the life of the believer and in the teaching of the community established to bear the historical revelation through history. This does not exclude the making of definitive judgments by those with the authority to make them. But the implications of even such definitive judgments, and the meaning and implications of the rest of the revealed message, come to be understood more adequately. Experience provides the matter for more differentiated insights into the principles of practical reason as well as into the data of revelation and the doctrine that rests upon and transmits revelation.[14]

A fine example of this process of developing reflective equilibrium is provided by the Second Vatican Council's Declaration on Religious Liberty (1965). This document, which repays study, identifies some of the soundest and steadiest foundations of the "public square" (and much more). It often goes by the first two words of its Latin text, *Dignitatis Humanae*—of the dignity of the human person.[15] Its core teaching can be stated quite briefly. All persons have a right, as individuals and as groups, not to be coerced by government either to perform or not to perform religious acts. This right is fully possessed even by people who hold false religious beliefs—indeed, even by individuals or groups who have formed their own religious beliefs without due care for truth. It is limited *only* by the needs of public order, that is, by the need to protect the rights of others and uphold public peace and public morality. The document divides its consideration of the right into two parts. The first defines, explicates, and justifies the right by reference to natural reason (i.e., natural law) alone. The second shows how it is rooted in Christian revelation and doctrine. The principal justifying argument from natural reason is this: *so important* is it for each human being to seek, find, and live according to *the truth* about God and man—religious truth—that coercion, which prevents, distorts, or tends to render inauthentic that search for religious truth, is wrongful. The wrong done is a wronging of the person whose search for truth, had there been no coercive pressure to conform, might have been authentic and centered on truth (about the most important things) at least as an aspiration, ideal, or goal. So that person (and thus any person) has the *right* (claim-right) correlative to the government's *duty* not to commit that wrong. And all this reinforces the document's further justifying argument, which recalls the classic Christian distinction between the secular and the ecclesial, and the idea (already coming to flower in Aquinas[16]) of limited state government: religious matters as such transcend the sphere of the state, and so "it would clearly transgress the limits set to [the state's] power, were it to presume to command or inhibit religious acts."[17]

The principal argument from revelation is this: God created human beings with the dignity, the elevated status, of rationality and freedom, and has added to that dignity by inviting all to share the divine life as his sons and daughters, an invitation which, for all who can choose, can only be fittingly accepted by a fully voluntary response:

> Redeemed by Christ the Savior and through Christ Jesus called to be God's adopted son or daughter, one cannot give one's adherence to God revealing Himself unless, under the drawing of the Father, one offers to God the reasonable and free submission of faith. It is therefore completely in accord with the nature of faith that in matters religious every kind of human coercion is to be excluded.[18]

The document treats as foundational for its newly accented teaching the historically continuous Catholic doctrine that no one can rightly be coerced into the faith:

> It is one of the major tenets of Catholic doctrine that one's response to God in faith must be free: no one therefore is to be forced to embrace the Christian faith against his or her own will [citations omitted]. This doctrine is contained in the word of God and it was constantly proclaimed by the

Fathers of the Church. . . . In the life of the People of God, as it has made its pilgrim way through the vicissitudes of human history, there has at times appeared a way of acting that was hardly in accord with the spirit of the Gospel or even opposed to it. Nevertheless, the doctrine of the Church that no one is to be coerced into faith has always stood firm.[19]

The underlying thought is this: reflection on historical experience leads the Church's teachers and members to the judgment that that doctrine—faith is not to be coerced—or its rationale, has wider implications. The authenticity and reality of the search for religious truth—and of the act of faith in which that search under ideal epistemic and volitional conditions would always end—are so prejudiced by threats of coercion that coercive measures for the sake of religious truth, whatever their apparent success, are self-stultifying and in opposition to the nature of human persons, because they are willy-nilly in opposition to the flourishing of human persons in one of its basic (and most overarching) aspects, the willing and thus whole-person-shaping *adhaesio* to God.

The natural law version (and so one might say the *economical* version) of the council's teaching is in the first part of the document, the fully *explanatory* version is in the second, or rather in the two parts taken together in their achieved equilibrium. Is the second part necessary? Cannot natural law and natural rights be affirmed confidently without the benefit of revelation? That is a question that I began to answer when I was pointing to the humanly necessary interdependence of natural reason and revelation. Consider, for example, equality.

That human beings are radically equal in dignity is entailed by the revelation that we are all made in God's image, and are called as sons and daughters into his household in the transcendent Kingdom.[20] Can we have much confidence that, without benefit of those revealed teachings, this radical equality would have been steadily understood and affirmed—practically, that is, precisely as ground for true entitlement of all to equality in basic rights—or much confidence that it will be long maintained if they are set aside?[21] I do not think so.[22] Without those revelatory insights, or confirmations of insight, into our nature and potential destiny, people—even people who understand human consciousness and character with the immense penetration of a Plato—gravitate toward some version of views that treat dignity as variable, waxing and waning, predicable of us at some time after the start of one's existence as a human being, perhaps at or perhaps quite a time after one's birth, and ceasing in "terminal" debility or disability. Or toward some variant of the view that human dignity is merely *ascribed* or *attributed*, not without flattery and speciesist bias, to beings whose true condition is like the other animals' and substances' in an indifferent universe, and whose claims and acknowledgments of rights are truly no more than conditions of peace affording a working basis for a life of comfort and satisfaction of desires while we may.[23]

Rawls's famous theory of political liberalism is that in one's decision-making as a citizen or public official, on matters of basic importance, one should never draw upon one's "comprehensive worldview"—one's deeper reasons for assenting to the principles and propositions that inform and direct one's decision. Instead one should proceed only on the basis of those reasons that are part of an overlapping consensus, in the sense that all (reasonable) people could reasonably be expected to "endorse" (that is "affirm" or "agree to"[24]) them. The theory is crippled by its ambiguity and unprincipled exception-making, as I and many others[25] better have shown. Anyone who thinks a proposition true thinks, or should think, that under ideal epistemic conditions all reasonable people would assent to it. So if it refers to ideal epistemic conditions, Rawls's radically ambiguous criterion—"all [reasonable] people can reasonably be expected to agree"[26]—excludes precisely nothing (except perhaps the opinion of those who think that value judgments are all relative and have no truth to them).

But if the criterion refers to the actual prevailing epistemic state of affairs, then it again excludes little or nothing, because Rawls accepts that reasonable people can and do hold some unreasonable views,[27] from which it follows that for all practical purposes there is no interestingly substantive view that *all* reasonable people agree to. So Rawlsian political liberalism's exclusionary principle rests on a mere double entendre, and once disambiguated proves quite empty. As for the arbitrary exception-making in his theory, one can see a good example when he envisages "rationalist believers" confronting what would otherwise (but for *their* beliefs) be a consensus. Helping himself to the assumption that "we" are inside this would-be consensus and the believer outside, Rawls says that we should simply draw upon our comprehensive worldview to declare the rationalist believers' belief either false or so undemonstrated as to be, in either case, ineligible to affect the consensus (without our judging that the believers themselves are unreasonable).[28] Here Rawls achieves his "consensus"-preserving exclusion by imposing on these rationalist believers a condition that he does not impose on "us," whom he never requires to be able to "demonstrate" any of our principles or positions to others.[29]

Rawls fails to take seriously the fact that "political liberalism" of his or any other kind may need to demonstrate its positions in the face of an existing or emerging antiliberal "consensus" or would-be consensus, not to mention the curious and the uncommitted. We may not be able to ignore this indefinitely, if large Muslim minorities or even, a bit later, majorities emerge in, say, European countries, and if these adhere, for whatever reason, to that important variety of Islam that teaches the legitimacy of forced conversion, expulsion of anti-Islamic views and practices from the public domain, and the capital guilt of apostasy from Islam.[30] Where is the defense of freedom of religious (including irreligious) expression and practice to come from? Even setting aside the unreasonable self-denying ordinances proposed in Rawls's theory of liberalism, where are we to find the bases for a defense of that freedom, or for a defense of the radical equality of men and women? Nowhere, I think, other—and certainly nowhere better—than from the developed Christian teaching. About that teaching, and the whole doctrine of revelation that underpins it, we have sufficient reason to be confident that its truth would be recognized under proper epistemic conditions of free and open minded discourse, that is, of public reason, properly understood and participated in—conditions that have scarcely been allowed to obtain in communities subject to Islamic rule.[31] If one should have that confidence in relation to a confrontation between Muslim and Christian claims to revelatory authenticity, one should, of course, also have it in relation to confrontation between the Catholic claims and atheistic or agnostic denials of them, denials which proceed from a position less reasonable than the Muslim (but also Christian) thesis that everything has its explanatory origin in the decision of the one eternal and all-powerful Creator. In this discourse between atheistic secularism and Christian secularism with transcendent foundations, what generally makes the epistemic conditions nonideal is not lack of political freedom from coercion but a complex of myths, images, and memories that block and distract from the Christian position and its evidences.

None of this is a prediction of what, in our world, will be the results of political freedoms of the kind that everyone has a right to participate in.[32] No one can foresee how the interaction between atheistic secularism, Islam, and Christian faith (with its affirmation of secularity alongside the sacred) will play out over this century—or foretell the interaction between development of doctrine and fundamentalism or radical orthodoxy within the competing sects in Islam.[33] Violations of rights[34] and of the other aspects of public order are indeed the responsibility of law and government to repress with judgment, equity, and an eye to consequences. But our reflections and inquiries should be directed not so much to speculations about the future as, rather, to fulfilling the duty that is the foundation of religious liberty, of morality itself, and of all decent political existence and coexistence: to seek the truth about God, and to follow it when one has found it as best one can judge.

6

Revelation and
Democratic Responsibilities:
A Comment on Finnis

Rogers M. Smith

The main point of John Finnis's eloquent essay is to argue, against John Rawls[1] and others, in favor of the propriety of making arguments from revelation in the public square, as part of "public reason." I write as an agnostic rationalist—a "comprehensive view" that, as Finnis argues, needs defense like any other. But I will not detail or defend my broader outlook here because on his central point I am wholly on the side of Finnis, and largely for the reasons he gives. All of us believe the basic tenets of our worldviews are ones that reasonable people would agree to under ideal epistemic conditions. But none of us can demonstrate this projected agreement to all the reasonable people who currently disagree with us, given that we do not and cannot live in ideal epistemic conditions, and given the likelihood that some of us, maybe all of us, are wrong. Therefore, neither Rawls nor anyone else has any right to privilege his own less than fully demonstrated moral principles while dismissing arguments from revelation as insufficiently demonstrated to be permitted as part of public reason. I have argued that such exclusions are politically impossible and that efforts to achieve them are counterproductive, spurring many believers to struggle to cast off "an uneasie and tyrannical Yoke," as John Locke contended in the first *Letter Concerning Toleration*.[2] But I also think these exclusions are morally wrong. They represent a claim to authority that has not been earned.

My comments will therefore not argue with Finnis but rather pursue four implications of this point on which we fundamentally agree. I suspect that I may see at least some of these implications differently from the way he does. But whether or not that is so, I think these are issues worth exploring, not least because on some points I am unsure about my judgments. The arguments offered here are meant not as final demonstrations of the rightness of my views but as contributions to dialogue with all those who are interested, however fundamental our disagreements may be.

Implications and Issues

In my book *Stories of Peoplehood*, I not only criticize Rawls for claiming that revelation is properly outside public reason, I go further and propose an alternative public ethos—one not of "public reason" but of "robust democratic contestation" among different explicitly, if at times economically, expressed worldviews.[3] I call this a Madisonian position, not because it derives directly from Madison but because it expresses a hope like the one Madison expressed specifically in regard to religion: if we permit robust contestation among different comprehensive views, the political exigencies of coalition-building may work to soften more extreme positions on particular issues and even to change minds over time, producing acceptable overlapping agreement on public issues without improper, counterproductive exclusions. This Madisonian view urges us to welcome religious arguments in public life, but it cautions believers that they must expect to have their religious claims challenged and criticized, not politely deferred to because they are matters of personal faith.

My position goes beyond Madison in part because I do not confine it to religion. Unlike, say, modern Germany, I would permit racist worldviews, as well as antidemocratic Marxist and fascist views, and openly irrationalist anarchist views, to contend in political arenas, believing and hoping that the champions of democratic processes would maintain enough support to prevent the most repressive forces from ever gaining power or from staying in power if they temporarily did. Religious believers like Professor Finnis might be more inclined to police the bounds of "public reason" than I am, even though we would both let in revelation—particularly since expression of the violent strains of Islam he rightly criticizes have produced destructive bombings in London. The first issue, then, is whether, even if the category of the "religious" is too broad to be placed outside the domain of "public reason," some worldviews should be. I argue not, but that position clearly has costs.

The second issue I wish to raise is a matter of specification. Finnis and I would both let revelation into the public square or rather keep revelation there—but on what terms? In American constitutional law, this is once again a vexed question today. The words of the Constitution, as well as our history, suggest that there is something special about religion, especially revelation-based religions, which requires special treatment by government. Article 6 bans religious tests for public offices; the First Amendment begins with a ban on establishing religion but also a guarantee of its free exercise. At least some of the Founders, and many American leaders since then, have felt that revelatory religious beliefs, which many saw as appeals beyond reason, were especially politically important and problematic—more likely to lead to human flourishing, perhaps, but also to uncompromising, dangerous zealotry. The two religion clauses of the First Amendment thus can be read as signaling that religion should be treated differently from secular moral outlooks. No religion can be established by the national government, so that government must sometimes distance itself from religious groups more than other types of groups. But because religious free exercise cannot be impaired by the national government, the religious may get exemptions from legal obligations that others do not.

Recently, religious advocates have argued with considerable success at the Supreme Court level that efforts to keep government from establishing religion have gone too far. They have therefore proposed an asymmetrical approach to the two clauses:[4] in Establishment Clause cases, such as issues of whether public schools and public locations should be open to religious student and community groups, they favor a principle of "equal treatment." Religious groups are welcomed on the same basis as any other, as they are perfectly legitimate civic organizations. Under the Free Exercise Clause, however, these advocates suggest that claims of religious conscience must receive special treatment—the state should defer to them in ways it should not defer to claims of secular moral conscience—since religious free exercise is distinctively specified in the Constitution, and since religion's special status makes this unique treatment appropriate.

As an agnostic rationalist, I find this combination unfair. The religious get equal treatment under the Establishment Clause, so they share equally in all public benefits, but special treatment under the Free Exercise Clause, so they get some benefits, some exemptions from state requirements, I cannot receive.[5] But I struggle over how to respond to this situation. The constitutional text does seem to treat religion as special, and religion may *be* special. So perhaps the answer is to treat religion as special under both clauses, making us especially wary of government's assisting religion in public programs—a position that can be taken to limit the role of appeals to religion in public policy debates, as in Rawls—while we should nonetheless be especially permissive toward claims of religious conscience.

My commitment to an ethos of robust democratic contestation makes me unhappy with the view of the Establishment

Clause that would result from treating religion as "special" in both these ways. Again, I would like to see religious arguments made in the public sphere as openly and as fully as their adherents can bring themselves to do. Those arguments should then be subject to contestation like any others. This same worldview also leads me to reject notions that my agnostic moral conscience should be publicly treated as less worthy of deference than those of religious believers.

I would prefer a policy of equal treatment across the board. After all, the Fourteenth Amendment added an equal protection clause to the religious clauses of the Bill of Rights, at a time when the country had moved decisively against formally established churches at all levels of government. I think that the religion clauses now must be read in light of that subsequent mandate for more extensive equal protection than U.S. governments had previously provided to citizens. I also believe that the First Amendment's own commitment to freedoms of speech and of the press, along with religion, points to the same conclusion. Historical experience may have made the Founders especially concerned about the political problems posed by religious belief, so they felt obliged to clarify its place specifically, but that does not show that they wished to give it constitutional superiority to rationalist moral perspectives or to make adherents of the latter second-class citizens. Still, as Robert George notes without putting himself in their ranks, many Americans across the political spectrum believe that the free exercise of religion does merit some sort of "preferred position" status above that of secular moral viewpoints.[6] So this is a second major issue that must be faced, even if we agree that religion should not be cordoned off from public reasoning.

Now the third issue. Though I think an ethos of democratic contestation points to equal treatment but not special treatment for religion, there is one regard in which I might be accused of favoring discriminatory treatment of religious arguments. The Supreme Court has frequently held that although a law may legitimately be based on religious reasons, it cannot be based on religious reasons alone. There must also be secular reasons that can legitimate the measure to nonbelievers.[7] Sunday closing laws may please the faithful and there is no harm in that. But those laws also need a secular rationale, as labor laws, as sources of a day of peace and leisure for the community.[8] Laws based on secular rationales, in contrast, do not need also to give a religious rationale. I have always supported this doctrine and so may be accused of not really favoring equal treatment.

My response is to say that, in principle, courts should be equally wary of both types of laws. They should give heightened scrutiny to laws that are supported by appeal to revelation but have no defenses in terms of practical reasoning on human nature or on the human condition, and they should give similar close scrutiny to laws that claim the latter sort of support but that violate the mandates of all or most of the religious traditions present in the political community. In each case, a law, even a democratically enacted law, will rest on rationales that many, though obviously less than a majority, find not only imprudent but deeply immoral and unjust. That is a highly politically problematic circumstance, to be avoided if possible. It is therefore prudent, indeed I would say a constitutional responsibility, for legislators not to enact laws that have a purely religious rationale, with no secular justification at all, or a purely secular defense, but with only condemnation from virtually every religious standpoint present in society. I question whether a law of either sort is likely to be minimally rational, even before we consider freedom of religion issues.

But in practice, in American society, only the first sort of law is ever going to happen, if indeed either is ever likely to happen. Americans are overwhelmingly religious, and it is simply impossible in democratic contestation for policies to win approval that find support in no significant American religious traditions— including broad though not unlimited abortion rights. Democratic political processes make sure that religious commitments always have some weight in American policy-making, a reality which seems fine to me though not to Rawls. But in an overwhelmingly Christian nation, there is still some possibility that religious majorities will pass laws that have strong support from revelation while having none from secular reasoning. Let me note that if John Finnis is right, this possibility should be seen as suspect even from a religious point of view. Practical reason, natural morality, and revelation are intertwined and mutually supportive, so there should in fact always be "natural" or secular practical reasons to give for measures supported by revelation. I think it is appropriate to ask that they be expressly stated in public lawmaking. In their absence, I would have American courts find an Establishment Clause violation; and this seems to me no great or unfair burden on religion. But again, it is an implication of a policy of welcoming religious views in public life with which not all religious adherents will agree.

The final issue I wish to raise concerns one kind of public religious discourse that does seem to me highly questionable, if not inappropriate, from the standpoint of an ethos of robust democratic contestation. This argument may regrettably seem partisan because I refer to the religious discourse that President George W. Bush had made central to his political as well as personal life. So let me stress again: I do not criticize President Bush for invoking religion or revelation in public discourse. I am glad that he did. I think someone seeking to exercise public power should make clear to his fellow citizens how and what he thinks. My objection is that President Bush's religious discourse was structured in ways to ward off, instead of invite, democratic contestation. Without specifying or interpreting its revelatory or natural bases, the president repeatedly led listeners to conclude that he had divine support for particular controversial policies, though he was careful never to say quite that; and he regularly suggested that embrace of his policies was a divine duty, so that critics were not merely wrong, they were blasphemous.

These are strong charges, so let me provide examples—noting that I often found Bush's speeches eloquent, even moving, although I objected to them. He structured his remarkable first inaugural address around a telling of "the American story" that culminated in the assertion "We are not this story's Author, Who fills time and eternity with His purpose. Yet His purpose is achieved in our duty; and our duty is fulfilled in service to one another."[9] Although this statement represented the sort of appeal to a religious comprehensive view that Rawls discourages, it was cast at such a level of generality that I at least did not initially find it disturbing. But this claim that Americans are not really the authors of their own political story became more worrisome as the president elaborated his providentialism in response to what are admittedly terrible dangers.

After the September 11 attacks, Bush both heightened his reliance on religious rhetoric and gave it increasing specificity in his major addresses and other statements. In his September 20, 2001, speech to the nation, the president identified Al Qaeda and Osama bin Laden as the perpetrators of the attacks and Afghanistan's Taliban regime as their protectors. He designated them the first targets in a new "war on terrorism." Bush argued that America was "called to defend freedom" and he concluded, "The course of this conflict is not known, yet its outcome is certain. Freedom and fear, justice and cruelty, have always been at war, and we know that God is not neutral between them."[10]

The theologian Caryn Riswold has expressed concerns about this speech consonant with my own. She argues that Bush's language inescapably suggests that his call to arms is "justified by God," whose sanction entitles Americans to "*certainty* of the outcome" of Bush's policies. She concludes that the speech "stakes a claim that America is the favored nation under God, and presents subtle justification for violence that begs for question, challenge, and serious criticism. It communicates a religious worldview that justified its veiled call for holy war, equating patriotism with faith in a God who is not neutral. The presidential address was a religious response, presenting a retribution theology as national policy, and communicating an arrogance that undermined its own power."[11] Again, I do not oppose political expressions of religious worldviews, and we cannot expect to end arrogant rhetoric. But Riswold is right to see in Bush's speech a confident assertion of certain religious authority for his actions that is unusual in modern presidential rhetoric.[12] Admittedly, it came in a moment of profound shock and crisis, when a nation needed to be rallied; but it soon became routine.

In his first State of the Union address, Bush stated that "history has called America" to "fight" and "lead" the campaign for liberty and justice, and he assured his fellow citizens that "God is near" to us amidst these difficult events.[13] On September 11, 2002, he reaffirmed that Americans had heard "history's call" and made clear that this was a providentialist history, saying, "We do know that God has placed us together in this moment . . . to serve each other and our country. And the duty we have been given—defending America and our freedom—is also a privilege we share. . . . This ideal of America is the hope of all mankind. . . . That hope still lights our way." Using explicitly biblical language, the president concluded, "And the light shines in the darkness. And the darkness will not overcome it."[14]

In his 2003 State of the Union address, Bush asserted that "this call of history has come to the right country," and he added that though "we do not claim to know all the ways of Providence," we knew enough of them to "trust in them, placing our confidence in the loving God behind all of life and all of history" as we pursued the course the president had set.[15] Later that year, in his important and widely praised speech to the National Endowment for Democracy, Bush argued still more explicitly that "liberty is both the plan of Heaven for humanity, and the best hope for progress here on Earth," and that as part of this plan, America had a "mission to promote liberty around the world." He concluded, "We can be certain that the author of freedom is not indifferent to the fate of freedom."[16] In his 2004 State of the Union speech, Bush argued that "God has planted in every human heart the desire to live in freedom," and he assured Americans that they would fulfill their "mission" to "lead the cause of freedom" because of "that greater power who guides the unfolding of the years."[17]

Then in his speech accepting his second presidential nomination, Bush returned to his motif of the "story of America," a "story of expanding liberty" in which "America is called to lead the cause of freedom" because freedom "is the Almighty God's gift to every man and woman in the world." He closed by assuring Americans that they "have a calling from beyond the stars to stand for freedom."[18]

Bush's Second Inaugural Address took as its central theme the argument that America must now make "the success of liberty in other lands" the centerpiece of national policy, for this task represented not only "the urgent requirement of our nation's security," but also "the calling of our time."[19] The president was careful to acknowledge that liberty might take different forms around the world, that "when the soul of a nation finally speaks, the institutions that arise may reflect customs and traditions very different from our own." The speech also contained passages that seemed mindful of criticisms of Bush's earlier providentialist rhetoric, as well as the example of Lincoln's great Second Inaugural, the latter of which recognized the divine justice of American suffering but refused to claim divine sanction for the Union cause, saying only that "the Almighty has His own purposes."[20]

Somewhat similarly, Bush stated that Americans had "complete confidence in the eventual triumph of freedom," but not because "history runs on the wheels of inevitability; it is human choices that move events." Nor did Americans "consider ourselves a chosen nation; God moves and chooses as He wills." Still, Bush insisted, "History has an ebb and flow of justice, but history also has a visible direction, set by liberty and the Author of Liberty." In his 2005 State of the Union address, devoted largely to domestic matters, Bush reiterated that Americans would "add to that story" of the "history of liberty," and that "the road of Providence is uneven and unpredictable—yet we know where it leads: it leads to freedom."[21]

These quotations leave little doubt that providentialist religious claims were central in George W. Bush's political discourse. But let me concede that, for all I know, these claims may be right; and again, I not only think the president had every right to express his religious convictions in public discourse, I found it clarifying when he did so. My complaint is in part that he did not tell us more. His rhetoric was consistently structured to support some quite specific policies by asserting that America has a calling to lead the cause of freedom worldwide, including striking where we suspect the presence of weapons of mass destruction. But how did he discern this will? What was the basis for his religious belief? Was it scriptural? His aides said Bush reads the Bible daily.[22] Was it a result of direct personal revelation, perhaps in his daily prayers? The president left these important questions concerning his invocations of religious guidance disturbingly unanswered when the answers might well have made a difference for the credibility of his claims. They certainly would have provided grounds for contestation.

Let me also acknowledge that Bush refrained from explicitly asserting that his measures were divinely authorized; his second inaugural eschewed the claim that Americans are a chosen people, and he more than once stressed that we cannot know all God's purposes and that, as an "almost chosen people," our "calling is to align our hearts and action with God's plan, in so far as we can know it."[23]

But his more restrained and qualified statements came largely outside his major official speeches, or, as in the case of his second inaugural, after the most controversial steps had already been taken. No reader of these quotations from the major speeches he had delivered when controversial policies were being first advanced can deny that President Bush frequently suggested strongly that his "war on terrorism" policies, including the war with Iraq, were in accord with God's will. I am sure that Bush sincerely believed this. But it should be equally clear that his speeches sought to make this confident belief audible to all, despite his care to avoid overtly claiming divine guidance for specific measures. As Riswold's critique indicates, these claims are controversial among those who regularly and openly take guidance from scripture, many of whom are pacifists. It is possible that the president preferred not to engage in scriptural justifications of his interpretations of divine Providence because to do so might invite theological quarrels. But to say that is to affirm that he structured his discourse so as to ward off full and open debate.

Perhaps his arguments about the providential course of history were really products of practical reasoning on the human condition today, reasoning that led to moral and policy conclusions that could be justified in secular rational as well as in religious terms. Though I doubt Bush would say that he did not in any way seek religious guidance in decision-making, he might well assert that his positions rested equally on secular rational grounds. He did often offer such reasons, though his major speeches frequently culminated in expressly religious assertions. If those religious arguments actually represented his decisive reasons, then they needed, I think, to be better explained and defended, not just asserted. But if they were essentially accompanying arguments directed to fellow believers, while he also gave secular grounds for nonbelievers, again, that seems to me a perfectly legitimate rhetorical strategy.

Yet even in that case, I remain concerned about how Bush's particular types of religious invocations were structured, about the message they sent to believers and nonbelievers alike. Though I understand the theological rationale, it seems to me questionable to stress in speeches to one's fellow democratic citizens that "we are not the authors" of the American story, especially when that claim is accompanied by repeated suggestions that pursuing administration policies is our "duty," our "calling from beyond the stars." Such arguments present religious legitimation as a substitute for accepting democratic responsibility—our own responsibility—for our policy choices. In fact, they logically suggest that dissent is a form of impiety, even sin. Religion here is being used, I fear, not to explicate, however economically, a political leader's positions. It is being used to sanctify by assertion, to issue authoritative mandates, and to discredit democratic discussion and disagreement. That, I submit, is not the proper role of religion in the discourses of the public square. At a minimum, the propriety of such rhetoric is a further issue that must be faced by all of us who wish to welcome religious arguments in public life.

7

Response to John Finnis:
Inviting More Explication and
More Economy

Eric Gregory

An ambiguous benefit of economic procedure (in the strict sense employed by Professor Finnis) is its capacity to leave interlocutors wanting more. Christian apologists welcome this opportunity with non-Christians even when the rhetorical aims of economy are met. The "economic" success of Finnis's clear and engaging essay is characteristic of his writings. But often those who share many of the religious and moral views expressed by an author—or merely appreciate their structure—are left wondering about the work that is being done by beliefs that are not made explicit. Explication need not compete with the discretion of economy, but understanding demands filling in some of the conceptual space that economy leaves empty. Such will be the tone of my response. I hope these remarks also will connect with some of the larger themes of this volume.

I have two lines of critical response. Both can be taken as friendly invitations and need not be taken as foundational disagreements. I here remain agnostic about whether or not these "further questions" can be postponed. I do think the approach taken in response to each would have large ramifications—both theoretical and practical—for the intersection of religion, morality, and politics.

The first line of response is theological. It is related to the important distinction between positive law and natural law, but it focuses more directly on the implicit status of the state and its relation to society or other possible forms of political community. My summary question is a familiar one in the history of Christian political thought, most recently revived by Protestant theologian Karl Barth.[1] Is the state essentially pagan? Or, to complicate the question, is the state a pagan invention that is somehow capable of making human persons less immoral, and thereby capable of securing some goods we would not otherwise have?[2] This question can be stated even more polemically. Despite his association of Protestantism with a declension narrative about Enlightenment secularism, is John Finnis really a Lutheran when it comes to his views of the state as a legal institution?

The second line of response is sociological. It has to do with the relevance of "telling the truth about God and man in a pluralist society." My summary question is a familiar one in recent discussions about public morality. Do we need a shared ethical *theory* to maintain a common morality? Here, in contrast to the first response, I am asking if Professor Finnis should be less explicit and more economical. I will focus this response in terms of the need to theorize human rights. Before pursuing these two lines of response, however, let me state some areas of deep agreement that motivate my interests.

Two Agreements

Despite their reservations about contemporary democratic culture and liberal theory, both John Finnis and Father Richard John Neuhaus find value in supporting the rights-based classical liberal democratic experiment conceived primarily in terms of the constitutional rule of law, that great hallmark of medieval Christian political thought. They also affirm the need for Christians to forge political friendships with those committed to liberal democratic institutions and practices. In so doing, they offer important alternatives to influential trends in contemporary Protestant social ethics that encourage Christians to imagine liberal democracy as a theological heresy, a trend that has begun to gain a foothold in some conservative Roman Catholic circles.[3] To the contrary, Finnis and Neuhaus characterize democratic citizenship as "an obligation and an opportunity."[4] Christian discipleship, for them, is not principally at odds with democratic citizenship. The source of this claim can be found in their mutual affirmation of what Finnis helpfully calls "Christian secularism."[5]

I share their sense of secularity as an essential element of Christian belief. Indeed, I think it is the crucial element that opened the door for the possibility of separating the political and the ecclesial without separating morality from politics or condemning the religious to private subjectivity. This possibility vexed Christendom, tempting it to close in upon itself and swallow politics with ecclesiology. For Finnis and Neuhaus, Christians rightly affirm an eschatological patience that gives creation room to breathe. This patience is not otherworldly resignation, but an affirmation of what *Gaudium et Spes* came to call "all that is good, true, and beautiful in the human community."[6]

The *secular*, in this sense, does not mean nonreligious or atheistic. It refers to the shared time afforded all humanity by the common grace of God. This conception rejects the sacralization of earthly political communities as vehicles of salvation. Liberal political society can be seen as a providential gift to be constructively sustained even when one denies the *secularist* claim that political communities are to be marked by moral neutrality.

This proviso raises my second agreement. I share Finnis's and Neuhaus's concerns about efforts to exclude religion from public life and the wholesale separation of law from morality. Maybe I am naïve and hopeful, or just bored with the narrowness

of its preoccupations, but I think the tide is turning on Rawlsian accounts of public reason. Critics rightly argue that these
accounts are undemocratic, unrealizable, politically self-defeating, and premised on a failed epistemology.[7]

Hopefully by the time we celebrate the fiftieth anniversary
of the *Naked Public Square*, we will be forced to hold a session
on "public reason" to remind students what it used to mean to
determine, in advance, what values and vocabularies should be
convincing to others in a free and open conversation about public
life. That said, I should add that I do not think it is appropriate
to cast John Rawls as the villain of modernity. I think, despite
concerns with the idea of "public reason," even here Finnis's essay
shares the morally informed spirit of Rawls's claim that "the zeal
for the whole truth" in politics is at odds with democratic citizenship.[8]

Finally, this is not the place to assess the merits of reading Aquinas's ethics primarily in terms of an account of "basic
goods" rather than virtue, or reading natural law as a moral theory rather than a theory of human action.[9] I do believe Finnis's
reconstruction has done much to revitalize natural law thinking
in ways that emphasize the richness of practical reasoning and
the centrality of freedom to human flourishing, but my response
does not enter into the deep waters of Aquinas interpretation. I
enter some other deep waters instead.

Theological Response

For Christians, the Incarnation is God's public reason. We rational creatures, beaten back by what Augustine described as our
false mode of resting in the world, need visible Wisdom to begin
our journey back home—even as we come to love this world in
God. Here from Book One of Augustine's *De Doctrina Chris-
tiana*:

How did He come except that "the Word was made flesh, and dwelt among us?" It is as when we speak. In order that what we are thinking may reach the mind of the listener through the fleshly ears, that which we have in mind is expressed in words and is called speech.[10]

Jesus Christ, I take it, is God's speech, God's visible witness. He is the highest good that is also the common good that elevates us into participation in the divine life. The witness of Christ continues in the preaching of the Church re-presenting Jesus as constituted in Word and Sacrament. The New Testament, notably Saints Paul and Luke, makes a big deal that all of this happened in the public realm, not hidden in some esoteric knowledge or contemplative inner voice.

Finnis points to this focal sense of publicity as the "heart" of his reflections.[11] In his book *Aquinas* he calls this communication from God to human persons "radically public and social in its making, in its transmission, and in its account of the point and fulfillment of life as individuals and groups."[12] This sense of public revelation, he argues, finds evidentiary force in the moral attractiveness of Jesus. While neither self-evident nor deducible from the self-evident, Christian propositions are rationally foundational to a sound intellectual life and "to fully appropriate public social institutions such as universities and states."[13] Drawing from such claims in his essay, Finnis also reminds us of the Church's powerful and articulate document on religious liberty, *Dignitatis Humanae.*

Now, here is my question: since the "good" of relating appropriately to a divine being can be "postulated without being affirmed,"[14] and inquiry into this good is an exercise in public reason, what does this entail in terms of the state's activities in relation to this basic good?

Finnis's account of Aquinas on the state is controversial. His Aquinas is not the Aquinas taught to most undergraduates, evidenced by his provocative claim that aspects of Aquinas's political thought are not readily distinguishable from John Stuart Mill's *On Liberty*.[15] His Aquinas sounds a lot like Augustine, or to be more provocative, what Lutherans take Augustine to be saying. The state is ordered to continence, not to true virtue. I think this view implicitly offers a third alternative to the debate between varieties of liberalism and communitarianism. Here we have a normative political community oriented to a public good, adjudicated by just laws, but limited in its application.

The state, conceived as a legal institution of judgment, is instrumental. Law does not promote true virtue or even inculcate virtues in its citizens. Rather, the state orders the public good, primarily it seems through promoting an imperfect tranquility, proscribing specific egregious external acts of injustice and (to the best extent possible) providing minimal conditions for human flourishing. Positive law is a cultural artifact, susceptible to all the sins of cultural artifacts, and therefore best focused on limiting harm rather than promoting good.

This state secures the space necessary for religion and the individual's pursuit of the life of virtue in community. Finnis commends the excellences that a liberal society makes possible, respecting the capacities of citizens as moral agents, and ordering life according to those things relevant to mortal life. The *polis* is concerned with the shared moral values appropriate to the penultimate, not with "soul-making." There is no radical separation of law and morality, but there is an important sphere of individual responsibility where the public good is not at stake.[16] Religious matters, Finnis claims, "transcend the sphere of the state."[17]

But is there something special about religion for jurisprudence given the state's interest in basic goods? Is the Christian Church something more than a voluntary society in the eyes of the state? What else does the state know about "religion"? For example, should the Catholic Church, since it promotes "religion" just as universities promote "knowledge," be eligible for tax-exempt status? If so, why? Is it appropriate for a nation to publicly recognize that its laws stand under divine judgment, and therefore collectively profess that the state is "under God," or to recognize its Christian heritage in a new constitution as an argument to deny admission to non-Christian nations? If so, why? Or, to take another example from the headlines, since the civil law may permit actions that are *malum in se*, is it plausible for a defender of someone with Finnis's views to argue that prudence suggests the state should withdraw itself from the legal regulation of sexual partnerships and confine itself to the contractual regulation of a variety of socially conferred benefits? Would this proposal thereby clarify the difference between a Catholic sacramental view of marriage from the pagan state's view? If not, why not? My confusion, and I stand to be corrected, stems from the apparent suggestion that the state does not just recognize claim-rights of religious liberty, but it also promotes the basic good of religion as one social form necessary to realize individual freedom, conscience, and vocation.

Here is the theological way of putting the question. Is the state pagan (as Anabaptists and sometimes Barthians say), unable to respond to the witness of the Gospel and not part of created nature that is perfected by grace? Or is the state under the Lordship of Christ and somehow analogously related to the order of redemption (as Calvinists like to say)? Or is the state in some third category, of the merely secular, belonging only to this passing age? If it is merely secular, as I think Finnis holds, then what is this state's relation to our final end? Nothing, it seems. There will be no political governments, no mediating institutions, in heaven. But, on Finnis's account, the government seems to know something about religion as a basic good, even as it remains neutral with respect to competing visions of this basic good. Religious conformity is not necessary for political stability. But I remain unclear about the status of religion. In short, there seems a tension between this account of the state and Finnis's account of religion as a basic good. Does the state only protect religion as a basic good, or can it ever promote it?

Sociological Response

For my second line of response, I shift from the theological to the sociological. Finnis argues that natural reason teaches that religious truth is so important a good that coercion is wrongful. Persons have claim-rights here correlative to the government's duty not to commit that wrongful injustice of violating religious liberty. Revelation further secures this teaching by introducing the notion that God created human beings with dignity, in God's image. Here he expresses doubt that, without benefit of this revelation, "this radical equality" would have become a ground for equality in basic rights. He speculates that if religious justifications are set aside, equality will not long be maintained. Without revelation, people gravitate toward some version of views "that treat dignity as variable, waxing and waning" or "merely ascribed or attributed."[18]

My question focuses on the sense in which he wants his readers to take these remarks. Are they pragmatic and speculative? That is to say, are they psychological remarks about the sociology of group adherence to the idea of equality? Or are they to be taken in some more robust sense? Put colloquially, do you need God to justify and maintain *human* rights rather than the mere rights of *citizens*?

If they are primarily pragmatic, I share his view that it is hard to imagine the development of human rights discourse in the West without the Christian tradition—in terms of both its beliefs and its social practices. If they are theoretical, however, I worry that he is placing a bit too much value on the need for a *shared theory* of human rights in order to maintain a workable common morality of human rights. Economic procedure, in this case, might warrant more theoretical austerity than Finnis appears to require.

The facts of pluralism do not lead me to skepticism about morality, but the power of my own self-deceptive emotional interests counsel me to always be on the lookout for potential ideological abuse of my favored ethical theory. Christians, as Finnis points out, are not immune to the distortions of rationalizations.

Very few people are skeptical about morality itself. Should not a natural lawyer think that particular moral disagreements often rely on deep moral agreement? Should not a natural lawyer trust the *demos* to play fair in the sandbox, ever ready to be surprised by virtue in strange places, even from those holding wrongheaded ethical theories?

Surely, there are a host of human rights theories and theories of equality that do not invoke the image of God that I think qualify as reasonable. But here is the real question. Do we need consensus on our justificatory theories of rights in order to maintain a world committed to radical equality and basic rights?

Where are we to find the bases for "a defense of radical equality of men and women"?[19] Finnis claims "nowhere better than from the developed Christian teaching."[20] I wonder, however, given the world in which we live, if we might better answer, "Wherever we can find it!" We do not need to agree on our theories of morality in order to sustain democratic practices and institutions. Does the moral health of democracy depend upon the adequacy of metaethical positions or reaching agreement on them? I hope not. Affirming this kind of political pluralism does not require affirming pluralism in one's theory of value or affirming moral skepticism. For Christians, in any case, we are interested not in protecting the bases of our ethical theories, but in protecting the neighbor that comes our way.

Christians are rightly concerned about the sorts of communities a liberal society tends to promote or encourage and the sort of social loss that Rawls himself admits. These problems are addressed by kinds of liberal perfectionism that I find attractive. With Augustine, I try not to expect too much or too little from politics. I do think it is a moral enterprise. We can work for a society with better loves than the ones we have now. But we can never expect true justice. All political communities fall short, but they fall short to different degrees. The better the objects of love—which entails recourse to justice—the better the society. I think religious traditions should help liberals imagine a better kind of liberalism and work to help their adherents be the sort of persons who work for justice in political communities. Such efforts do not demand recourse to an account of "basic goods" or unanimous consent on any given ethical theory.

In many ways, I think we are conscious of standing at the end of a long march of democracy and liberalism, or at least that democracy and liberalism associated with the European Enlightenment and early modern political philosophy. I think liberalism has achieved amazing results, making possible the kinds of lives that we are able to lead. But, like many ages of transition, it requires a moral imagination, a refashioning of inherited traditions, and the inculcation of social virtues necessary to face an uncertain future.

In the end, though Aristotle may have thought that you need a morally upright culture to become moral, Christians, Thomists, Augustinians, and Lutherans should hold otherwise. There is always and already grace. That is something that delivers us from more than our capacity for sound moral reasoning, not as a cheap quick fix, but in the training, directing, correcting, healing, and even perfecting of the gift of virtue that Christians claim to find in the law of Christ.

8

Religious Pluralism and the Limits of Public Reason

William A. Galston

Introduction

In the course of preparing for this conference on which this book was based, I reread two books I had not touched for nearly twenty years. The first was an issue of *Daedalus* on the topic of "Religion in America," published in 1967. To open this volume was to enter a vanished world. The lead article was Robert Bellah's famous essay on civil religion. Pondering the sources of contemporary American Protestant theology, Langdon Gilkey, professor of theology at the University of Chicago's Divinity School, discussed (inter alia) science, history, self-fulfillment, the social gospel, existentialism, phenomenology, and linguistic analysis. (He noted in passing that many devout laymen had been "profoundly shocked" by the notion that the creeds of their church were expressions "relative to the time in which they were written."[1]) For his part, William McLoughlin, a professor of history at Brown University, took note of the upsurge of activity among fundamentalists and religious conservatives but dismissed the phenomenon as a radical right fringe whose weakness had been dramatized by the collapse of the Goldwater campaign. McLoughlin opined that

> If by a third force one means a force that is capable of significantly altering a culture or that is symptomatic of a significant new shift in the dynamics of a culture, then neither those who call themselves "the Conservatives" (or neo-evangelical or fundamentalists) in America . . . are a third force.[2]

Instead, he suggested, the Will Herberg triad—mainstream Protestants, Catholic, and Jews—was most likely to play that role. While there were some dissenting voices, confidence in the liberal-progressivist vision of our religious future suffused this volume with little awareness of the conservative-traditionalist countercurrents that even in 1967 were growing in self-awareness and strength.

The second book I reopened after a hiatus of decades was *The Naked Public Square*. The book I encountered was not quite the book I remembered. I see more clearly now that Neuhaus was waging a two-front war against moral majoritarian fundamentalism (now clearly a rising political and cultural force) as well as aggressive secularism. He advocated a principled via media, an account of Christianity as "public truth" accessible to "public reason."[3]

In the intervening two decades, the issue of public reason has been intensely debated, largely under the influence of John Rawls. When I returned to Neuhaus's work, I was surprised to discover that his account of public reason bears more than a passing resemblance to Rawls's. Neuhaus criticizes the religious new right for "*making public claims on the basis of private truths.*"[4] The integrity of politics, he says, requires us to resist all such proposals. Public decisions, he insists, must be made through arguments that are "public in character." He continues, "A public argument is transsubjective. It is not derived from sources of revelation or disposition that are essentially private and arbitrary."[5] Accordingly, those who want to bring religiously based values into the public square "have an obligation to 'translate' those values into terms that are as accessible as possible to those who do not share the same religious grounding."[6]

I will note, but not dwell on, some of the unavoidable ambiguities of this thesis. In the first place, the phrase "as accessible as possible" elides as much as it clarifies. How much inaccessibility—that is to say, privacy or subjectivity—is acceptable (if any)? Acceptable to whom? Mathematical proofs are in one sense (in principle) accessible to all—in practice, not so. I take it we would not want to exclude economic arguments from public discourse just because most people lack the training (and many the capacity) to evaluate their merits. Many will wonder whether the analogy between economics and religion is a good one: the (partial) inaccessibility of faith-based values has nothing to do with inequalities of training or rational capacity but is rooted, rather, in orientations and experiences that not all do (or can) share.

Second, it is not evident a priori how much of what is distinctive about "religiously based values" gets lost in translation. The more fully a particular faith embraces a natural law perspective, the less is lost. Because different faiths divide on their orientation toward natural law, the translation requirement will have a disparate impact. For that reason, some will regard it as a less than fair or neutral principle—put more pointedly, as a Catholic assault on certain kinds of Protestantism.

Third, it may be argued that different sorts of discursive standards are appropriate for different kinds of public claims. For example, a faith-based claim to be exempted from otherwise binding law need not be as fully transparent as a claim that the entire political community should comply with a specific faith-based value. The former claim is defensive and particular; the latter is offensive and general. When the children of Jehovah's Witnesses seek to be excused from saluting and pledging allegiance to the flag in public schools, they are not required to defend their belief that such behavior amounts to religiously forbidden idolatry. The bare fact of the belief warrants the exemption, or so I have argued.[7] It would be a different matter altogether if a group invoked religiously based prohibitions against charging interest in an effort to change financial legislation affecting everyone.

These are ambiguities in, but not objections to, Neuhaus's account of public reason. The real difficulty lies elsewhere, in what I regard as an excessively unitary account of reason or (what amounts to much the same thing) excessive confidence in reason's power to resolve our deepest differences. Neuhaus raises the stakes by equating pluralism with "indifference to normative truth."[8] There is an alternative account of pluralism, however, that affirms an objective (in Neuhaus's language, "transsubjective") account of morality, as follows: The distinction between good and bad is more than a variable human contrivance, but goods are multiple, heterogeneous, not reducible to a common measure of value, and not definitively rank-ordered. Human reason can rule out certain courses of action or states of affairs as intolerable, indecent, or inhumane. But after what is unacceptable has been excluded, reasonable people can and do differ about what to affirm, and there is no neutral authority to resolve these disagreements.

The stakes are higher still if one simultaneously affirms a unitary account of reason *and* brings religion under the canopy of reason. This is what I understand Neuhaus to have done in *The Naked Public Square*. In its strongest form, the rationality of religion thesis suggests that reason suffices to decide the issue between (say) Christianity and Judaism. This stance is reminiscent of the assumption underlying medieval disputations among faiths, such as the one so memorably imagined in Judah Halevi's *The Kuzari*.

Among many other difficulties, this thesis is contestable on theological grounds. Within Judaism, the faith-tradition I know best, it is customary to distinguish, as Maimonides does, between religious commandments reason is fully competent to justify and others, the force of which is rooted, at least in part, in revelation. The former constitute a kind of generic religion of reason, which some scholars regard as the Jewish version of natural law. But the latter define the beliefs and practices that constitute the distinctiveness of Judaism.[9] My impression is that most other faith-traditions embrace some version of this distinction and that many define a scope for reason narrower than that in Rabbinic Judaism and, by extension, much narrower than the strong natural law position Neuhaus appears to embrace.

This theological problem is likely to spill over into politics if divisive issues of law and policy turn out to rest on religious differences, rooted in what faiths regard as authoritative revealed truth, which reason cannot adjudicate. I shall devote the next section of this essay to an example of this kind of intractable disagreement.

Biotechnological Controversies

One of the most remarkable recent events in American religious life is the formation of what I call a traditionalist entente linking theologically conservative or orthodox believers across ancient divisions separating Protestants, Catholics, and Jews. On a wide range of issues involving public values, these traditionalists have joined hands against liberals within their own faiths. Against this backdrop, when Baltimore's William Cardinal Keeler participated in an ecumenical forum to discuss the ethics of cloning, he was surprised to find that in contrast to his own prohibitionist stance, shared by the forum's Protestant representatives, the Orthodox rabbi refrained from issuing a blanket condemnation of the practice.[10] To be sure, other Orthodox Jews reassured the prelate that their brethren were not unanimous on the issue. (No surprise: have Jews ever been of one mind on any issue?) But had Cardinal Keeler been moved to inquire further, he would have found that the rabbi had spoken for the mainstream of Orthodox

Jewry and that his accommodationist stance toward cloning was rooted in the fundamentals of Jewish theology. Let me try to explain.

I take as my text a statement on cloning issued in 2002 by the Orthodox Union, a group involved in public policy advocacy on behalf of the Orthodox community. It reads, in part, as follows:

> Our Torah tradition places great value on human life; we are taught in the opening chapters of Genesis that each human life was created in God's image. After creating man and woman, God empowered them to enter a partnership with him in the stewardship of the world. The Torah commands us to treat and cure the ill and to defeat disease wherever possible; to do this is to be the Creator's partner in safeguarding the created. The traditional Jewish perspective thus emphasizes that maximizing the potential to save and heal human lives is an integral part of valuing human life. Moreover, our tradition states that an embryo *in vitro* does not enjoy the full status of human-hood and its attendant protections. Thus, if cloning technology research advances our ability to heal humans with greater success, it ought to be pursued since it does not require or encourage the destruction of life in the process.[11]

This statement sets forth, in highly compressed form, a number of propositions that are central to the Jewish outlook. The first is a distinctive religious anthropology. In the Jewish tradition, man as the "image of God" is understood not as contemplative, not as suffering, but rather as creative, indeed, as a kind of co-creator. Neither God's law nor nature is simply given or passively received; each is to be developed through human agency guided by human reason.

A famous Talmudic passage encapsulates the stance of Jewish orthodoxy on the interpretation of divine law. A number of rabbis were debating a fine point of ritual. Rabbi Eliezer took a stance in opposition to the others. When his arguments failed to persuade them, he called for a series of miraculous signs, each of which came to pass in support of his view, but the other rabbis remained opposed. Finally he said, "If the *halachah* [law of the Torah] agrees with me, let it be proved from Heaven." Whereupon a heavenly Voice cried out, "Why do you dispute with Rabbi Eliezer, see that in all matters the *halachah* agrees with him?" But Rabbi Joshua replied, "It is not in heaven" (a quotation from Deuteronomy 30:12, referring to the Torah). The Talmud continues (characteristically) by posing and answering a question: "What did he [Rabbi Joshua] mean by this?" Said Rabbi Jeremiah: "That the Torah had already been given at Mount Sinai; we pay no attention to a heavenly Voice, because Thou hast long since written in the Torah at Mount Sinai, After the majority must one incline" (a reference to Exodus 23:2).[12]

While this Talmudic brand of magical realism may seem odd, the meaning of the tale is straightforward: while the Torah is the fruit of divine agency, its interpretation and application to specific issues is a matter for human reason guided by experience and common sense. On matters of binding law, God's intervention in human affairs ended at Sinai. The rest is up to us—that is, up to judgment by the majority of those whose learning and wisdom renders them competent to pronounce judgments.

It is to be expected that the mutability of human affairs will produce new problems, such as biotechnology, that the written law does not explicitly address. What can be thought of as Jewish common law arrives at judgments on such matters through the application of standardized interpretive techniques and modes of legal argument, including arguments by analogy. (In such circumstances, of course, scholars may disagree whether a new phenomenon is more like A, which is permitted, or B, which is forbidden.)

Jews see the relation between nature and technology as similar to that between the Torah and what I have called Jewish common law. In each case, human agency is not only permitted but also commanded to shape what God has given. Man's dominion over nature means that nature was designed for human use. Jewish Orthodoxy is incompatible with an aesthetic or contemplative environmentalism, or with any worldview that places man on the same plane as the rest of nature. This is not to say that human beings are free to use nature in any way they choose. There is, for example, a Talmudic prohibition against "witchcraft," defined as the effort to harness unnatural powers to malign purposes. According to Maimonides, however, anything for which the association of cause and effect is established by accepted scientific rules falls outside this prohibition, however startling the products of action guided by scientific innovation may appear.[13]

With regard to intent, Rabbi Kenneth Waxman summarizes the tradition as follows: "When human creative capacities, ingenuity, and technology are utilized to alleviate suffering or to improve the human condition even in the broadest sense, our actions are permitted, perhaps even mandated, and constitute a full-fledged accomplishment of the religious ideal of *imitatio Dei.*"[14]

A second key theological premise at work in the statement of the Orthodox Union is the high value placed on healing the sick and alleviating their suffering. In this respect, among many others, Judaism emphatically rejects an otherworldly orientation: one's fate in the afterlife, however fortunate it may be, is no substitute for life and health, here and now. So important are these goods that their pursuit trumps what would otherwise be prohibitions: doctors may violate the Sabbath to save lives, and individuals may break even the fast of Yom Kippur if their health demands it.

The third key theological issue concerns the status of the embryo. In unfolding the meaning of the Orthodox Union's statement, I rely on the authoritative exposition of Rabbi Yitzchock Breitowitz.[15] The following are the central points:

1) The Talmud distinguishes between an embryo prior to the fortieth day and those that develop past that point. A number of

otherwise binding legal requirements do not apply to a woman who miscarries before the fortieth day of pregnancy. Accordingly, serious genetic defects or medical problems that do not endanger the life of the mother may justify abortion during this period.[16]

2) According to Rabbi Breitowitz, a pre-implantation embryo should not be entitled to more *halachic* protection than a pre-forty-day implanted embryo, and there are grounds to afford it less. Thus, "if genetic testing uncovers a defect which would justify abortion of a pre-forty-day embryo, destruction of the preembryo may be similarly permitted." Many, though not all, contemporary authorities go farther, permitting the destruction of so-called surplus pre-implantation embryos even when the actual abortion of the same embryo, once implanted, would be forbidden.[17]

Rabbi Moshe Dovid Tendler summarizes the classical Jewish position in the following terms:

> The Judeo-biblical tradition does not grant moral status to an embryo before forty days of gestation. Such an embryo has the same moral status as male and female gametes, and its destruction prior to implantation is of the same moral important as the "wasting of human seed". . . . The proposition that human hood begins at zygote formation, even in vitro, is without basis in [Jewish] biblical moral theology.[18]

It might well be thought that this stance is morally risky because it may lead to a slippery slope at the bottom of which is the taking of human life. The Jewish tradition is sympathetic to this line of argument. Indeed, much of rabbinic law consists in the effort to build a protective outer perimeter (a fence) around the law of the Torah. For this reason, says Rabbi Tendler, Orthodox Judaism respects the effort of the Vatican and fundamentalist Christian faiths to erect fences that will protect the biblical prohibition against abortion. But a fence that prevents the cure of fatal diseases must not be erected, for then the loss is greater than the benefit.[19]

The three propositions I have discussed—human agency as the image of divine creation, the imperatives of curing disease and saving life, and the moral status of the preembryo as less than fully human—lead Jewish orthodoxy to endorse a range of stem cell research that involves therapeutic cloning. As Rabbi Tendler puts it, "In stem cell research and therapy, the moral obligation to save human life [is] the paramount ethical principle in biblical law" that "supersedes" concerns for the preembryo.[20] And even when materials intended for life-saving therapy are drawn from acts that Jewish law forbids, including many abortions, the Jewish tradition does not forbid their use: "An illicit act does not necessarily result in a prohibition to use the product of that act."[21]

From the standpoint of traditionalists in other faiths, these positions are unwelcome and surprising. More surprising still, Jewish orthodoxy is far from implacably opposed to reproductive cloning. In the course of a comprehensive review of Jewish law on the subject, Rabbi Michael Broyde notes that there do not seem to be any "intrinsic halachic grounds to prohibit cloning," and that there are some circumstances in which it may be deemed acceptable. For example, in the Jewish tradition, one of the core commandments is to be fruitful and multiply, a requirement that is especially binding for men. If a man is unable to fulfill this commandment through any means other than cloning, then reproduction through cloning is not only permitted but also commended.[22] Moreover, Broyde observes, the Jewish tradition "would not look askance on the use of cloning to produce individuals because these reproduced individuals can be of specific assistance to others in need of help." So there is nothing wrong with having a child through cloning to provide a life-saving bone marrow transplant; our motives for reproduction can be mixed without ceasing to be legitimate.[23]

Let me translate this discussion from the language of theology and divine law to that of moral philosophy. If one uses the familiar distinction between deontology and consequentialism to categorize Jewish Orthodoxy, one would have to say that Orthodox ethics is closer to the latter. Jews experience the force of affirmative obligations to produce the greatest amount of good, and Orthodoxy endorses few absolute side-constraints respecting that which would limit the ability of human beings to maximize the good. As Barry Freundel, an Orthodox rabbi, puts it, "Human beings do the best that they can. If our best cost/benefit analysis says go ahead, we go ahead. 'G-d protects the simple' is a Talmudic principle that allows us to assume that when we do our best G-d will take care of what we could not foresee or anticipate. If things do not work out, the theological question is G-d's to answer; not ours."[24] By contrast, John Cardinal O'Connor succinctly formulates the deontological stance of canon law as follows: "Is cloning human beings morally permissible? Categorically no."[25]

Political Consequences of Religious Pluralism

The point of the preceding section was not to offer a primer on rabbinic theology but rather to underscore a simple contention: orthodox faiths that unite in resisting religious liberalism and modernism may nonetheless disagree about the content of theology and about its social implications. The question is how this fact should influence our understanding of the appropriate public role of religion. I can sharpen this question by posing what appears to be a conundrum: If, as Neuhaus insists, religion should shape public life, including public law, through the exercise of "public reason," then it would seem that the content of public reason is in principle accessible to the adherents of all faiths equally as well as to those who espouse no religious faith. If so, then it is hard to see how religion, as opposed to philosophical natural law, is playing any distinctive public role. On the other hand, if the content of a specific revelation is to play that role, it can only be by breaching the boundaries of public reason as Neuhaus defines it.

Lest the abstract formulation of this conundrum deprive it of argumentative force, let me be concrete. As we have seen, traditional Catholics have one understanding of the moral status of early-stage embryos, traditional Jews quite another. It is possible, I suppose, that unaided reason can settle this dispute, but the disputes of the past thirty years offer little evidence that this is so. It is more likely that the differing orientations toward the embryo of these two great faiths represent disagreements rooted in the fundamentals of their respective theologies.

To find a public resolution, one might try to appeal to something between reason and revealed theology—namely, our everyday moral experience. Alas, this changes the venue of controversy without resolving it. Consider, for example, the outcome of the deliberations of President Bush's Council on Bioethics. While the ten-member majority of the council favored a moratorium on cloning for biomedical research, a seven-member minority would have permitted such research under suitable regulation. A noted conservative scholar, James Q. Wilson, joined the dissenters. His justification rested on an account of moral experience:

> A fertilized cell has some moral worth, but much less than that of an implanted cell, and that has less than that of a fetus, and that less than that of a viable fetus, and that the same as of a newborn infant. My view is that people endow a thing with humanity when it appears, or even begins to appear, human; that is, when it resembles a human creature. The more an embryo resembles a person, the more claims it exerts on our moral feelings. Now this last argument has no religious or metaphysical meaning, but it accords closely . . . with how people view one another. . . . This fact becomes evident when we ask a simple question: Do we assign the same moral blame to harvesting organs from a newborn infant and from a seven-day-old blastocyst? The great majority of people would be more outraged by doing the former than by doing the latter.[26]

No doubt others have different moral sentiments and (even if Wilson were right about the moral majority's view of the matter) would deny the relevance of counting heads to answer such questions. But that is exactly my point: while moral experience may provide an essential point of departure, it speaks with an ambiguous voice. (For the record, I note the suggestive resemblance between Wilson's account of our moral sense and the stance of traditional Judaism.)

The implications of this apparently intractable disagreement for public law are stark. If the law permits the practices of stem cell research and therapy that traditional Jews believe should be allowed, then acts will proliferate that offend the beliefs of traditional Catholics. On the other hand, if the law bans what Catholics believe to be intolerable, then it will prevent Jews from acting in ways that they consider commendable and, in some cases of dire emergency, mandatory.

What is to be done? One argument, which I advance with hesitation for discussion, takes as its initial premise the old Jewish principle that "anything for which there is no reason to forbid is permissible with no need for justification."[27] The second premise of the argument is that to justify coercive public law across the boundary of diverse faith communities, only what Neuhaus terms public reason counts as a reason to forbid a practice. By contrast, for individual faith communities, propositions based on specific revelation that are shared by the members of those communities but not by nonmembers rightly serve to justify morally and institutionally binding prohibitions within those communities.

This argument takes its place within a pluralist understanding of the relation between faith communities and the political community. Through coercive public law, the political authority creates a framework that requires uniformity only on those essentials that public reason can justify. The remainder of the social space is filled by diverse communities, faith-based and secular, that enjoy the liberty to order their internal affairs based on their distinctive understandings of human purpose and ultimate meaning. Further, members of subcommunities can request, sometimes demand, exemption from otherwise binding public laws when these laws command what faith or conscience prohibits or prohibit what faith or conscience demands.

Clearly this stance requires each subcommunity to accept the possibility that other members of their political community will act in ways that they find morally or religiously offensive, unless they can justify their moral or religious views through the exercise of public reason. For many, this counsel of restraint may seem to ask too much. But in circumstances of deep moral and religious pluralism, I find it hard to imagine an alternative that would not be worse.

Part Three

Conclusion

9

Looking Back from 2034:
The Naked Public Square—
Fifty Years Later

Hadley Arkes

It is an honor and no small achievement to be here to celebrate the fiftieth anniversary of Richard Neuhaus's book, *The Naked Public Square*. For here we are now in 2034—in the middle of centenaries of the New Deal—and who would have thought so many of us would be here to mark the occasion?

Of course, while this is the fiftieth anniversary of that enduring book, *The Naked Public Square*, it is now the thirtieth anniversary of the journal called *The Naked Public Square*; and I took it as a mark of his large nature that Richard never interposed objections when some of us founded a new journal, taking the name of his classic book.

But the book *The Naked Public Square* certainly stated the problem in a jolting way, and the curious thing is that the problem, over the next twenty years, seemed to become notably worse. The scholarship supporting Richard's argument was being reinforced with each year, with Philip Hamburger (*Separation of Church and State*), Michael Novak (*On Two Wings*), Daniel Dreisbach (*Thomas Jefferson and the Wall of Separation between Church and State*), and James Hutson (*Religion and the Founding of the American Republic*) all showing the religious understanding that was pervasive at the Founding.

The Founders never expected, never even imagined, that the laws could be purged of any reference to the Creator who endowed us with rights—when that was the understanding that pervaded the laws. As the understanding ran, no man was by nature the ruler of other men in the way that God was by nature the ruler of men, and men were by nature the ruler of horses and cows. It was entirely salutary, as Madison suggested, that citizens in a republic would already begin with a respect for a law outside themselves as a preparation for respecting the laws. As Jefferson famously put it, nothing stood above the ruling majority . . . except for the moral law. But that is what made the profound difference between a people constituted as a political people and a criminal band. A people bound by the moral law understand that they may rightly command, in the name of their authority, only rightful things. They recognize, in other words, that they have no "right to do a wrong" even in the name of their sovereign authority. And for the same reason, they had no right to do a wrong even to themselves. They understood, that is, the things they had no right to claim, even in the name of their freedom and their rights. But to speak of the moral law was to point outward to the Author of the moral law—as Hamilton put it, that "superintending" authority, who "has constituted an eternal and immutable law, which is, indispensably, obligatory upon all mankind, prior to any human institution whatever."[1]

To Hamilton, Adams, and James Wilson, the awareness of that Author of a moral law was the assurance of a moral law that would not be suspended when governments broke down or were awaiting formation. It would have been a burlesque then to suggest that this understanding of God was entirely a matter of *private* belief. The understanding was nurtured in a *communal* teaching, passed on from generation to generation; it was developed with argument and the canons of reason accessible to people, which is to say, a *public reason*. And it had an inescapable public significance, especially in the life of a republic. Richard wove this theme through *The Naked Public Square* in making his plea that the religious tradition could not be pushed to the periphery in the private sphere, where people may savor, in closeted settings, such curious things as pornography.

Richard put in place in *The Naked Public Square* the ingredients for the argument he would make more fully in his essay in the journal *First Things* "Can Atheists Be Good Citizens?" It was not, of course, that atheists could not be decent people who obeyed the house rules, the traffic laws, along with the other laws set down in the positive law. A good citizen, in the deeper sense, is the citizen who could give an account of the moral premises of that regime in which he stood as a citizen. He would be in a position then to offer a *moral* defense of that regime, and of the rights it was meant to secure. That is not an office that can be taken up in our own time by people who insist, with Nietzsche, that God is dead and everything is permitted. As part of the Jewish-Christian tradition we have brought forth, of course, a tradition of natural law. We can reason in a principled way about the things that are right and wrong without appealing to matters of faith. But recall that line from Mr. Justice McLean in his dissenting opinion in the *Dred Scott* case: that black man was not chattel; he was a creature who "bears the impress of his Maker, and is amenable to the laws of God and man; and he is destined to an endless existence."[2] He was made, in other words, in the image of something higher. My colleagues, people of large liberal sympathies, understand that they cannot quite give the same account of the wrong of the Holocaust and the wrong of slavery that McLean was in a position to give. But that is to say, they start by ruling out any ground on which to say that the people around them have an intrinsic dignity, then, the source of rights of an intrinsic dignity that the rest of us need be obliged to respect. The question that Richard has planted, so critically, is the question of just who or what does the heavy lifting done by the God of Israel, or the God who endowed us with rights, if we begin by banishing that God from any founding premises in our moral judgments or our laws.

The Constitution detached from religion, the Constitution that would push religion out of the public square, was a rather late invention. It came with the clever statecraft of Hugo Black in 1947, and the measure of the success of this project is that people came to think that it was ever thus. And yet, even as other scholars joined Richard in showing that it had not been thus, the political class in control of the courts seemed to move on, unaffected, not to be diverted. And so, a youngster in a public school, receiving aid to the deaf under the laws of the United States and Arizona, would lose that aid when he shifted into a Catholic school (a judgment reversed in *Zobrest v. Catalina Foothills School District*). We would be told in *Lee v. Weisman* that it was a matter of "coercion," subtle, psychological coercion, if a student were merely expected to sit in silent respect while others offered the mildest prayer to the God of Christians and Jews. Symbols of native religions could be placed in public parks, but not crosses, not the Ten Commandments.

We should have known that things were ebbing for us when Merchant and Ivory thought we were sufficiently historical that they could make a movie out of *The Naked Public Square*. That, of course, did not work out. But they were misled by their remarkable success in making a movie out of the *Critique of Pure Reason*. No one thought it plausible, but for some unaccountable reason Meryl Streep seemed to touch a wide audience as she played the Second Analogy and did Kant's answer to Hume. It was probably a mistake when she was replaced by Bernadette Peters and they tried to do the *musical* version on Broadway, but that seemed to everyone to be overreaching. As Louis Armstrong complained about be-bop, people complained of the musical version of the *Critique of Pure Reason*: no one sang it, no one danced to it.

The more plausible project came when Merchant and Ivory thought they would do a film of the Neuhaus Circle, or the Family, as we came to know it, as a kind of mixture of the Bloomsbury

Group and the Oxford Movement. After all, Richard had managed to bring together in this circle, at times, people who found it hard to be in the same room together. But the core of the group, the people who truly formed the family, seemed to be bound by this enduring affection and attachment. As several members had remarked—and everyone readily confirmed—nothing in these meetings ever seemed to be lost. Things said four or five years earlier would be recalled by others as they bore, with force, on the point at hand. No one let anyone get away with anything, with any argument that was frivolous, and yet the corrections, when they came, came with affection and with a brotherly humor.

The first discordant notes came, as I recall, not in any theological dispute, but in certain minor irritations over who would play whom in the movie. Gwyneth Paltrow as Midge Decter we all thought was just out of bounds. But Judy Holliday had died long ago—someone Jewish, feminine, tough, funny. It wasn't too bad when they fixed Dustin Hoffman up with glasses and had him play Robert Wilken. But William Powell had long ago died, and so we did not have someone of that urbanity and dash to play Jim Burtchaell. They could never get anyone right for Robby George or for David Novak, and I bridled at Ron Silver to play me because he had played Alan Dershowitz in one movie, and I was constantly irritated at being mistaken on the street for Dershowitz. But what could I do? Jody Bottum represented a real problem. But then it seemed to come as an inspiration: Father George Rutler, to play Jody. Quite uncharacteristically, Father Rutler showed some hesitation. Could he spin out a learned discourse, woven with literary allusions and passages from the Bible? Of course he could do that and with the same nonchalance. Could he leaven all of this a bit with references to some recent, dense works in theology? And could he make a bit of theater of it by having that discourse trail off into passages so refined that they acquired a comic edge? Yes, yes, of course, he allowed he could do all of that. Then what was the hesitation? Well, he wasn't sure that he could do all of that while at the same time keeping a stream of languorous, seductive smoke coming from a chain of cigarettes kept constantly lit.

But that problem was just another reflection of the lovely implausibility of characterizing this rollicking, brilliant band. John Cardinal O'Connor seemed to catch the sense of this back in September 1991, when Richard was ordained in a ceremony at Dunwoodie, and we were all there. The Cardinal said, in those memorable words, "Richard, you don't deserve this, any more than I deserve to be here ministering to you and presiding." But as O'Connor took in the scene, even he seemed to be struck by the fact that he was not getting only Richard; he was getting a whole ensemble. Henry James once described a Sunday evening in St. Peter's square, with the pageantry—but also with the vendors and the gossip, as though everything in the world was brought within its compass. And as he said, the walls of this event were nothing short of the walls that encompassed this vast Church of the world, which "has no small pruderies to enforce."[3] Something of that kind must have impressed itself at once on Cardinal O'Connor, who was so quick and savvy. Something like that must have occurred also to Cardinal Law back in Boston. At a pro-life dinner in the 1990s he asked someone to bring me up to be introduced, for he wondered how I could write all those pro-life pieces domiciled, as I was, in Amherst. But he quickly got to the matter of his deeper curiosity and interest: he was sure that I must be coming into the Church, and he thought, surely, that when Richard came, I would be coming too. I told him that this had been in fact quite on my mind, but that the rest of us thought that, when Richard came over, he had arranged a "group rate" for his friends.

But those were the heady days, when we had absorbed Richard's legendary hopefulness. The political class was growing more and more hostile to the religious tradition, and that hostility would find its sharpest, most venomous reflection in the campaign against George W. Bush in the election of 2004. If anything, the hostility was not abated, but sharpened, as the election came without a resolution, and the litigation kept going in five states even after November 2. The administration that took office later, as a coalition, with Dennis Hastert and Joe Lieberman, could be assembled mainly by putting religion and the moral questions at the periphery of our politics. Those kinds of concerns would be understood now, more surely than in the past, as quite distant from the main concerns of politics, which involve taxes and regulation. Looking back, we see it was but another stage in the decline of a serious commitment to religiosity—until the breakthrough of recent years, with that unexpected revival, that Great Awakening Redux.

Richard always saw the bright side. Christianity seemed to be eroding with churches being turned into museums and malls everywhere in Europe, except for Poland, and yet America still seemed to be the most religious country in the world. Even in Seattle, in a state so liberal and hostile to religion, Rabbi Daniel Lapin had noted that one could drive about on Sunday morning and see the parking lots filled at all of the churches. But while the signs of religiosity were indeed widely spread, the question that kept gnawing at us was whether the reality was just pathetically thin. I recall that, at Amherst, the flourishing of the gay and lesbian issue on the campus seemed to intimidate the Evangelicals and Catholics and induce them to preserve a decorous silence. But the chilling sign for me came, as I remember, one evening in April 2004, when my college had sponsored a busload of students going to Washington to affirm their support for abortion rights. In response, a group of students, organized by the Christian Fellowship, arranged to hold a candlelight vigil on the campus on that evening to mark the concern for unborn children destroyed in the growing casualties from abortion. But as we were gathered that night, the designated leader and spokesman, offering prayer, voiced his hope for the day when abortions in the country would become "less necessary." "Less necessary"? Some of us looked at each other with quizzical faces: where did this come from—who talked us into this? (Could we not have done something to make it "less necessary" to get rid of the Jews in Germany in the 1930s? Could we not have found some healing device for transferring Jewish businesses into the hands of deserving, Aryan owners?) We would learn later that one of the organizers of the Christian Fellowship had written a piece for the student newspaper, assuring people that while the fellowship had a deep lament for the lives taken in abortion, the leaders in the fellowship were mainly pro-choice on the matter of the laws, for they did not wish to impose their own religious beliefs on others with the force of law.

Were the Evangelicals getting flaky? Or was it simply a reflection of the people drawn to a college such as Amherst—or Wellesley, Williams, Brown, Wesleyan, Harvard, or Yale? But you see the point. The country was moving into enclaves. The serious Christians and Jews could be found mainly in schools that were avowedly sectarian—though even many of them felt the need to accept the lesbian rabbi or the gay minister in training as a way of showing their tolerance or their large natures. But at the same time, the so-called secular schools were becoming even more sectarian; they were becoming ever more emphatic in drawing moral lines, in denouncing inequality and racism, and in affirming the rights of women. And they became, with each step, even more strident and emphatic in proclaiming their moral sentiments—even while they insisted that nothing in their moral judgments claimed the standing of truths.

Looking back, we can see the issue of gay rights sharpening in a trend moving over eight years: there was *Romer v. Evans* in 1996 on gay rights in Colorado, followed by *Lawrence v. Texas* in 2003 on the laws on sodomy; but then the movement really came to the point of crisis, the point of judgment, in Massachusetts in 2003 and 2004, when the Supreme Judicial Court installed same-sex marriage as nothing less than a constitutional right. These were the moves that drove the culture war over the edge. More than anything else, that matter of gay marriage established the hegemony of the Left in the culture and in our politics, as we found that we could not break the hold of the courts and their allies in the political class, sustained by the media and the "best schools" in the country.

In retrospect, it was curious that so many people, otherwise savvy about the world, and tutored in law, failed to see those lessons that Lincoln had taught with such preeminent clarity about the logic of morals itself. Lincoln had offered a kind of restatement of Aquinas when he used that logic of morals to bring out the implications of Stephen Douglas's position and explode his clever finesse. Douglas would affirm the holding of the court in the *Dred Scott* case, that people had a right not to be dispossessed of their property in slaves when they entered a territory of the United States. But then, to his followers in the North, he would offer the assurance that they could refuse to honor that right if they withheld the regulations and laws needed to support the right not to be dispossessed of property in slaves. As Lincoln would later put it, Douglas was saying that "a thing may be lawfully driven away from where it has a lawful right to be."[4] By the logic of morals, after all, if there was a "right," then anyone would be obliged to respect that right and support it. No one holding office in the United States could be warranted then in casting up impediments rather than sustaining something now stamped as a constitutional right.

Lincoln brought out that logic of morals quite as well in his famous address at the Cooper Union in February 1860, where he brought out also what we may call the darker side of rights. Lincoln remarked that, "if slavery is right, all words, acts, laws, and constitutions against it, are themselves wrong, and should be silenced, and swept away."[5] If he agreed that slavery was morally right, then he could indeed grant the demands of the slave states to have the abolitionist message censored and screened out of the federal mails. As it turned out, activists in the cause of gay rights, or gay and lesbian marriage, seemed quite attentive to this logic of rights—and quite alert to the implications that spring from it. At the same time, most members of the public, and almost everyone in the media, seem to be utterly uncomprehending of it. Consider the translation: if there is something legitimate and rightful about the gay-lesbian life, and there is nothing less than a constitutional right to have same-sex marriage, then anyone who would resist it, anyone who would cast up impediments to it, is doing something wrongful. Anyone who would call that kind of marriage into question may be, in certain settings, a wrongdoer inflicting harms and portending deeper injuries.

In that vein, I recall myself that, at a hearing in Boston in the spring of 2001 on our version of the Defense of Marriage Act for Massachusetts, a Unitarian minister argued that anyone who would favor the Defense of Marriage Act and openly resist the rightness of gay marriage was engaging in nothing less than a hate crime. In his considered estimate, that kind of speech opposing gay marriage was likely to license hatefulness and stir others on to violence against gays and lesbians. Not long after that, in August 2003, something called the Irish Council on Civil Liberties put out a warning that "clergy and bishops who distribute the Vatican's latest publication describing homosexual activity as 'evil' could face prosecution under incitement to hatred legislation."

In what became our famous Symposium on Judicial Usurpation in the late 1990s, I had recalled, in my own piece, a good friend of mine, a senior partner in one of the most prestigious law firms in New York and a serious Catholic. He had been quoted in a trade paper among lawyers when he expressed his dubiety about laws that moved in a sweeping way to ban all discriminations based on "sexual orientation." This senior lawyer was dropped from the recruitment committee of his law firm before it was sent out to recruit at the law school at Harvard. And the rationale was rather clear: The senior partners at a law firm will pass on the hiring and promotion of young associates. If the corps of senior partners contained people who are affected, already, with an adverse judgment on homosexuality, then the complaint can be lodged that the situation is rigged from the outset, or at least tilted against the associate who is gay or lesbian. And so the very presence in the firm of partners of someone with a moral judgment against homosexuality meant that there would be already, from the beginning, a condition that makes plausible the filing of a grievance. From that possibility, now sharpened, there came into sight the prospect of some vexing, expensive litigation.

Law firms are nothing if not responsive to incentives. And so the inferences were quickly drawn: the very presence in the firm of people with rather pronounced moral and religious views on homosexuality would make the firm deeply vulnerable to litigation. Firms would find an incentive then to foreclose the problem at the very threshold by the simple expedient of avoiding the hiring of people who were—shall we say?—"overly religious." In *Romer v. Evans* in 1996, Justice Antonin Scalia already noted the tendencies in this direction that had been expressed in the rules of the Association of American Law Schools. As Scalia noted, interviewers at the law schools could turn away applicants because of all kinds of prejudices that had nothing to do with their competence to practice law: whether they were adulterers, as Scalia said, whether they ate snails, went to the wrong prep school, wore real animal fur, or hated the Chicago Cubs. But one prejudice was regarded as so preeminent that it had to be condemned with a special force: in the bylaws, then, of the Association of American Law Schools, it was specified that the schools would have to extract from all firms interviewing at their schools a pledge of their willingness to hire homosexuals.

Now all of that was in place before the Supreme Judicial Court in Massachusetts established for the state nothing less than a constitutional right to same-sex marriage. But with that step, the politics of this issue was moved into an entirely different register for the whole country. It did not require all that much imagination to see the steps that would spring readily from the moves already taken. It required merely that awareness, once again, of the logic of morals, as the motor that would drive the process forward. Anyone who grasped that logic could readily see what might be called the Dark Side of Rights as that scheme began to play itself out. Yet that Dark Side remained remarkably invisible, or out of sight, to people who had no sense of how rights in the law were connected to a moral logic of rights.

We fall here again into the fictive anticipation of things yet to come. The first steps came in the fall of 2004, then through the academic year 2004–5. They began, of course, in Massachusetts, for Massachusetts stood now, conspicuously, as the only state in the Union that offered a legal enclave for same-sex marriage. As some of us foresaw, the gay-lesbian law students at Harvard passed a resolution affirming their pride, first, in the example set by the state of Massachusetts in taking an advanced position on same-sex marriage. It was then resolved that firms sending their representatives to Harvard to recruit young associates should reveal just how many members of their firm would reject the legitimacy of gay marriage and how many would support the claim that the traditional laws on marriage were indeed unconstitutional. For as the argument would go, to invite gay and lesbian students into a firm containing people with serious scruples against homosexual marriage would be to invite them into a firm that was critically biased, from the outset, against their retention and promotion. Of course, the question was being posed without the force of law by students at a private university. But once the faculty came to adopt the position of the gay and lesbian students, the firms would be barred from access to one of the most prestigious law schools in the country and the source of some of the most promising young lawyers.

It should not have taken high powers of conjecture to see that the same resolution adopted at Harvard would quickly be imitated at Yale, Duke, Columbia—and from there sweep to other law schools dominated by faculties already massively tilted to the side of favoring same-sex marriage. After that, things played out in a path that, once again, should have been easily predictable. The stance taken in the law schools quickly spread to the other schools and divisions of the leading universities and colleges.

Along a parallel track ran resolutions passed by the professional associations feeding the academy: the American Psychological Association, the American Political Science Association, the association of historians, and others began to adopt comparable resolutions. And one could see right away the lessons that were being taught to people entering graduate school about the lines of orthodoxy being established. Students were quick to pick up the signals on the kinds of people who could expect to be hired. They could gauge rather quickly what their prospects would be for jobs in the academy if the titles of their dissertations did not emit the correct signals and if the students still harbored sentiments that put them out of alignment with the orthodoxy now entrenched on the campuses.

All of this was taking place, again, in private arenas, with private colleges and professional associations. But of course the movement had been showing its sharper expression in the public arena, where the laws came more explicitly into relevance. The Boy Scouts, with their articles of opposition to homosexuality, had been barred from the use of public parks in certain liberal cities. Now the move to bar them swept from coast to coast, and it would spread then to bar from public facilities and programs those churches that retained their traditional teaching on sexuality and marriage. Vouchers approved for religious schools would already carry a provision barring their use in schools that discriminated on the basis of race. But now the ban was extended to schools that might after all, in their teaching, teach disrespect and contempt for the rights of gays and lesbians to enter into marriage with persons of their own sex.

Those kinds of exclusions would burgeon, and they are too numerous to detail here. But it is worth recalling that they were given their most important fillip when the activists used as a powerful lever the holding in the famous Bob Jones University case from 1983.[6] In that case, as you may recall, that fundamentalist school was stripped of its tax exemption under federal law because the school, in its private rules, barred marriage and dating across racial lines. Of course, no one had been denied access to the school on the basis of race, and there had not been a complaint in that respect lodged against the school under the Civil Rights Acts. No laws on racial discrimination had been violated. On the matter, then, of dating and marriage, the school was an association of private persons who shared the persuasion that they should confine their dating and marriage within racial lines. That might be illiberal, and yet curiously the principle of discrimination had never been conveyed in the laws: states could not bar interracial marriage in their laws, but private persons were still left free, in their own private judgments, to prefer people of their own race. Some of us pointed out at the time that it was only in the journals of liberal opinion—in journals such as the *New York Review of Books*—that one could find ads in the "personals" column reading "SWM seeks SWF." Translation: single white male seeks single white female. The *New York Review* would never have run an ad saying, "white landlord seeking white tenant." The upshot, unmistakable, was that the most advanced section of liberal opinion did not think that it was wrong for people, in their private choices of partners in sex and marriage, to prefer people of their own race. Nevertheless, the Supreme Court agreed with the curious claim that the policies of Bob Jones University ran counter to the "public policy" of the United States—even though, as I say, there was no such public policy of the United States: there were no statutes or executive orders that barred people, in their private choices, from preferring to marry people of their own race.

But when the Supreme Court of the United States, in 2013, held that there was indeed a constitutional right to marry people of the same sex, there was indeed now a doctrine in our law, a doctrine that would have to be regarded as fundamental in our public policy. And with that point established, the activists would drive it home. Any church, any religious group, any fraternal group that included in its teaching or in its articles of association an adverse judgment on homosexuality would be stripped of its tax exemption. This move swelled into a campaign, and the campaign had the effect not merely of making certain churches and parishes unsustainable, but also of inducing many churches to shade their teachings, to back away. But that in turn invited the aggressive moves of dissidents within those churches to push for the overthrow of the old teaching, much in the way that important parts of the Anglican and Presbyterian movement had come to adopt gay marriage even without this kind of prodding.

As George Marsden recalled in *The Soul of the University*, there was a strategic move by the Carnegie Foundation in 1906 to cover the pensions for the faculty in the colleges if the administrations of these colleges would detach themselves from the last ties of denominational control. In that way the schools would be lured into breaking the last ties that connected them to their religious origins, their character, and their original missions. A bit over a hundred years later, in 2015 Mr. George Soros would resume that task of transmuting through grants. In the name of his late professor, Karl Popper, Soros would offer grants to colleges that would purge themselves of their chaplaincies and the vestiges of a reactionary, religious sensibility. In his settled view, those atavistic religious outlooks were always threatening to block the commitment of the college to the fullest "rational" inquiry. Soros would take his lead from the patrons who sponsored lectures and departments on "peace studies." He would sponsor groups committed to throwing over any lingering religious restraints on such projects as research into the use of embryonic stem cells. With the backing of Soros there began to appear on the campuses new, richly funded projects on "The Breakthroughs of Science," "Science Unbounded," and "Science Liberated from Superstition"—a science that would be free, as the saying went, from retrograde religious views.

Here, we revert again to the factual record, though it turns out to be even more fantastical than the simple, sober projections of the future from what we had seen already in our experience. That the possibilities were rich here was a matter signaled dramatically by the American Academy of Religion as it assembled the papers for its meeting late in 2004. The academy had been founded in 1909 as a means of bringing together scholars who taught religion in universities and colleges. A mere glimpse at the abstracts of the papers was enough to show a profession that was now not only detached from the religious tradition, but virtually at war with it. And so Professor Justin Tanis of the Metropolitan Community Church offered a paper entitled, "Ecstatic Communion: The Spiritual Dimensions of Leathersexuality." Professor Tunis explained in the abstract:

> This paper will . . . look briefly at the ways in which leather is a foundation for personal and spiritual identity formation, creating a lens through which the rest of life is viewed. . . . All of this is based within the framework of a belief in the rights of individuals to erotic self-determination with other consenting adults, rather than apologetics for those practices and lives.

At the same conference, Professor Ken Stone of the Chicago Theological Seminary remarked that a passage from the book of Jeremiah (20: 7–18) "can be construed more usefully as a kind of ritual S/M encounter between the male deity Yahweh and his male devotee." Finally—for my examples, not as an exhaustion of the papers—Professor Kent Brintnall of Emory University offered a paper on "Rend(er)ing God's Flesh: The Body of Christ, Spectacles of Pain, and Trajectories of Desire." This paper, he said, "substantiates [note—substantiates] the claim . . . that sado-machochistic [sado-masochistic?] homoerotic desire is part of what makes the spectacle of the crucifixion attractive and desirable."

I could go on, but the time is short, for we are, after all, operating under a curfew, and we must be finished by 10 p.m., so that we can be off the streets by 11 p.m. That thought itself draws back some ironies of the past. The liberals, in their early ACLU phase, resisted policies that would bar people from going door to door, or stopping people on the street, to press a religious or political viewpoint. But the change came in response to the pro-life movement, when the liberals thought it was legitimate, however, to stop people from approaching women entering an abortion clinic, or even praying outside the clinic, lest the gesture imply a reproach and inflict hurt. As things heated up in the argument over gay marriage, the first move was to bar people from wearing certain hateful signs of opposition to these new rights. But that is to say, any sign of opposition was regarded as hateful, and likely to stir the violence of people who (it must be said) quickly did become violent. The matter was worsened, of course, outside of bars or ballparks in the evening, and soon the ban was made explicit there. At a certain point, administrative neatness required people to stop engaging in these encounters at a specified time late at night.

Back in 1968, when Congress banned racial discrimination in the sale or rental of housing, the administrators were quick to respond to the efforts to evade the law with advertising using allusions and subterfuge. And so people were barred from putting up ads on bulletin boards or trees advertising a racial preference, and they could not use such devices as saying, "Apartment available, near St. Aloysius Church" (or "near Itzkowitz's Delicatessen"). That was a form of "signaling." Well, little did we expect that even innocent gestures would suddenly run afoul of the same techniques. After same-sex marriage went through . . . well, marriage just seemed to lose the sense of what was special about it. Weddings with trappings, weddings in churches, seemed to many overblown, for to put it another way, marriage itself was brought down to earth. Marriage was not for a lifetime, not for children; it could be evanescent. In short, it was not exactly any longer, as they said, a "big deal." In response, some parents and fiancées began to put on their invitations that they were inviting their friends and relatives to a "real marriage" or a "marriage as of old." But curiously, these practices were challenged and then barred by the law, much in the same way that the law had barred those ads with the references to St. Aloysius or to Itzkowitz's Delicatessen. And so it became an offense for anyone to put out an invitation or a notice in the newspapers about a "real marriage"—much in the way that ads implying racial or ethnic discrimination had been barred from bulletin boards or trees or any public setting—for such language was taken to denigrate the marriage of gays and lesbians as things that would not stand as "real marriages" in the same way or on the same plane of legitimacy.

With the same sensibility, schools and associations were not allowed to disguise their religious character simply by taking on another name. In the words they would use to advertise themselves or their purposes, they too would fall into signaling, whether they referred to "traditional" or "classic," or called themselves the New Boy Scouts, as a jazz band could call itself the New Black Eagle. None of this was availing. And when it became expedient simply to bar religious groups from having their members on the streets past eleven o'clock, the curfew was extended even to groups such as this one, tonight, which does not bear in its title any religious reference. For the subject alone, taking up the work of Father Richard Neuhaus in his notable book, lamenting the state of religion in our politics and public discourse—that was quite sufficient, you see, to indicate just who we were.

I would offer a summary word, then, on the trend I have described, but then, quite in the style of our friend Richard Neuhaus, ever hopeful, I would mark the signs to be welcomed in our own time, the signs also of hope for the future.

The summary word is that the trend of events I've recounted here tonight shows us again the way in which the teachings and compulsions of the law move from the public realm until they spill over into the private realm as well. We began with the leverage of the law in pressing home the logic of enforcing a new right. As of old, the law would attach penalties—and stigmas—to those who could be labeled now as wrongdoers. The right proclaimed at the top of the state by the courts works its way out then from the public to the private. It begins with the things that public agencies may not endorse, may not legislate. It moves to the things that public agencies may indeed legislate, in spreading this new right through the public domain. And then, this new conviction of rights is allied to the levers of the law in spreading its regulations into private settings—to the corporation, the college, the small business. At a certain point this new sense of the law, this new sense of rights, begins to affect the kinds of things that people feel free to say, without hazard, in their most private settings: colleagues must be careful as to what they say to one another, lest even bantering remarks become the ground of litigation. And finally that sense of caution, or serious danger, imparts a certain guardedness in what people dare to say even to their own children. They must take care that things said in private settings are not artlessly repeated in public settings, where they can draw trouble for the children and notoriety for the family. In these ways, subtle and unsubtle, definite and firm, the people who form the regime establish their rule most emphatically by establishing the things that it is no longer respectable or safe to say in public. And as this trend reached its fullest expression, the public square became even more naked and hostile than the public square portrayed by Richard Neuhaus in his famous book.

Well, that has been our story for a long while. But as ever there have been strands of hope. And in every case in which a country drifts into nihilism or systems of perverse judgment, the main hope has come through conversion. After all, we have seen conversion change the lives of persons, and if it can change some, it can change many. It *has* changed many. The most notable hope has come from the emergence of a kind of Oxford Movement, but centering, of all places, on Princeton, that enclave of a lapsed but once flourishing Presbyterianism. In this new stirring, there were two remarkable agents. In a campus torn by many implacable divisions, Luis Tellez, at the Witherspoon Institute, was one of the few figures who could talk with virtually everyone across the spectrum of that campus. He would draw to its activities the religious among the faculty and students, and draw them in across the divides—he would draw in Evangelicals and even Orthodox Jews along with Catholics. And in the classroom, as a magnet, as a prime example and a source of attraction, there was the inimitable, unsinkable Robert George. In the early part of the century, it was already detectable: young members of the faculty making their way to Mercer House because they were interested in Catholicism. The movement would soon connect some of the most brilliant members of the faculty with some of the most gifted students. They were here in a critical mass, students who were in the top rank, smart, handsome, quick of wit, religiously serious, politically conservative. From Princeton, with the seed, the plant has grown, and spread itself with offshoots and seeds in other places. That plant will not be readily torn up, even now, for the people in this movement seem to draw strength from the fact that they are standing against the world, or against a culture grown pagan, but a pagan culture without the redeeming intellect of a Plato or Aristotle.

Charles Rice, at Notre Dame, used to buck me up when I was especially glum about the pro-life movement, and he would say, "Don't forget, you're on the winning side." There was a conviction about the way in which things would come out at the end. And that, over the years, seems to have been Richard's conviction just as well. He has been ever, and maddeningly, hopeful. Even in the darkest times, he sees the hidden lights, or the aspects, the sides that reflect the good planted in human nature, or the capacity of human beings to reach outside themselves to something divine in their nature. History has meandered, and meandered mainly for the worse, and yet at every stage we have been persistently drawn back to that plea of Augustine that Robert Wilken kept drawing us back to years ago. We are called back even now, and from that source we continue to draw hope. And so, we persistently hear Robert's voice, speaking those lines to us as ever from Augustine. We buoy up our friends, and we appeal to those open to conversation, as we say again, "[W]henever you are as certain about something as I am, go forward with me; whenever you hesitate, seek with me; whenever you discover that you have gone wrong, come back to me; or if I have gone wrong, call me back to you. In this way we will travel along the street of love together as we make our way toward Him of whom it is said, 'Seek His face always'" (Psalm 105:4).

10
Afterword

Richard John Neuhaus

The first word is a word of thanks to Robert George, Christopher Wolfe, and others responsible for putting together this lively conversation.

Any writer must be gratified when a book is deemed worthy of such conversation two decades after its publication. Calvin is supposed to have said to a friend, "Today I have sent a book off to the printer, there to perish like a beautiful rose dropped into a very deep well, never to be heard from again." Such is the fate of most books, although, it should be noted, not of Calvin's.

The Naked Public Square is an argument. Like most arguments, it had to wait its time to get a hearing. My hunch is that books that become something of a point of reference appear at the edge of a time when a lot of people are already persuaded of the argument but have not quite put it together. Then comes along a book that elicits from readers what the sociologist of knowledge Alfred Schutz called an "Aha! experience." "But of course," they say. "That's just what I've been thinking."

To be sure, those who are unsympathetic to the argument are more likely to say, "That's just what I suspected *they* were thinking." It is important to understand who was the "we" and who the "they" in the writing of *The Naked Public Square*. In preparation for the conference on which this book is based, I went back and reread the book in its entirety for the first time. It was as I thought, and as several participants in this conversation have pointed out. The authorial voice is typically pitched to the "we" of people familiar with the intellectual history and practice of liberal democracy. They were then, and, for the most part, still are, liberals of one kind or another. The then-emerging "they" was what then was called and is still called "the religious right." The book was in large part a response to the question "What are 'they' saying that 'we' got wrong, and what should be done about it?"

Twenty-five years later, many of those who were once "they" are now "we." The growing public influence of politically engaged conservative Christians has frequently been accompanied by an immersion in the theory and practice of democratic politics. Theirs is no longer simply an aggressive defense against those who once made up the rules that excluded them. Twenty-five years ago, the very phrase "religion and public life" was highly controversial. In that combination, they were fighting words. Today, as Mary Ann Glendon notes, there are numerous institutes, academic centers, and publications established on the almost taken-for-granted premise that we cannot understand this society or sustain this polity without engaging the cultural and religious dynamics that shape the "We, the People" that is the locus of political sovereignty.

As many of the former "they" are now "we," so also many of the "we" are less worried about being viewed as "they." Those who are most militantly committed to the ideology of the naked public square have of late taken to raising alarms about the threat of "neoconservatives," "theoconservatives," and even of "theocrats." This is for the most part the last gasp—although it may be a very long last gasp—of those who would deny the self-evident truth that this constitutional order is not sustainable apart from the cultural, moral, and religious expression of the self-evident truths on which it is founded. Of course, I may be wrong about that. That denial may yet prevail. The Founders regularly called this order an experiment, and experiments can fail as well as succeed.

The reemergence of religion in our public life will always entail the danger, just as critics charge, of people imposing their moral judgment on others. Democratic deliberation leads to decisions, and decisions backed by law are viewed as an imposition by those who disagree with those decisions. So it has always been. The charm of democracy is that most decisions are for the time being, and those who disagree will get their innings. Democracy is not only procedural, and the procedural itself rests upon the foundation of commitment to certain moral goods, but it is very importantly procedural. The procedure is less about imposing than about proposing and persuading, and thus arriving at provisional resolutions in the form of a political equilibrium that is always for the time being.

How we propose and persuade raises the question of "public reason" that came in for much attention in our conversation. Were there time, I would want to address William Galston's distinction, indeed near dichotomy, between public reason on the one hand and religion and revelation on the other. I am persuaded that we live in a universally graced creation in which human reason participates in the mind of God and is capable of ascertaining moral truth and making moral arguments accessible to all reasonable persons.

This, too summarily stated, makes possible the kind of natural law reasoning so elegantly proposed by John Finnis and others. While ideal epistemic conditions are seldom obtained, most, if not all, of the questions pertinent to politics in a limited state ought to be resolvable by moral reason—whether or not called natural law—that is accessible to all.

In the aberrations and contingencies of the world as it is, however, I am inclined to be skeptical about the possibility of agreeing on clear rules in determining what counts as public reason.

Short of the Kingdom of God, it is probable that we can at best arrive at a kind of modus vivendi that will not satisfy the intellectually fastidious. Thus I am sympathetic to Rogers Smith's call for "robust democratic contestation," in which moral reason and natural law arguments play an important part. Here I find myself in agreement with Eric Gregory when he writes:

> Where are we to find the bases for "a defense of radical equality of men and women?" Finnis claims, "nowhere better than from the developed Christian teaching." I wonder, however, given the world in which we live, if we might better answer, "Wherever we can find it!" We do not need to agree on our theories of morality in order to sustain democratic practices and institutions. Does the moral health of democracy depend upon the adequacy of metaethical positions or reaching agreement on them? I hope not. Affirming this kind of political pluralism does not require affirming pluralism in one's theory of value or affirming moral skepticism. For Christians, in any case, we are interested not in protecting the bases of our ethical theories, but in protecting the neighbor who comes our way.[1]

I suppose some may think that smacks of intellectual cynicism. Others, intending it as blame, may say that I am more of an Augustinian than a Thomist, and there is something to that. Ours is a fallen world in which reason is not just wounded but wounded to the point of corruption, albeit, thank God, not total corruption. By reason we entice from reason the best of which it is capable, knowing that undisciplined passions will time and again deprive us of reason's full fruit. Meanwhile, in this robust democratic contestation, we avail ourselves of whatever reasonable arguments, popular aspirations, rational fears, and motivating visions—so long as they are not dishonest or debasing—in order to achieve a closer approximation of justice, which is the virtue most proper to politics.

The word meanwhile is critically important. As the letter to the Hebrews reminds us, we have here no abiding city but live toward the promised New Jerusalem. Christians and Jews who share that hope form a band of happy warriors without illusions. Hadley Arkes does well to remind us of the words of St. Augustine: "Whenever you are as certain about something as I am, go forward with me; whenever you hesitate, seek with me; whenever you discover that you have gone wrong, come back to me; or, if I have gone wrong, call me back to you. In this way, we will travel along the street of love together as we make our way toward Him of whom it is said, 'Seek His face always.'"[2]

This is the pact of truth and love that binds together those who seek His face always while seeking here on earth what justice may be possible. Not everybody seeks His face, and many, in both theory and practice, despair of justice. In the robust democratic contestation, we never forget that, in the words of St. Paul, we are also contending against the principalities and powers of the present disordered time.

In "East Coker" Eliot writes, "For us there is only the trying, the rest is not our business." These are words not of resignation but of gratitude. We are not God. Thank God we are not God. In the long run of history, when the experiment that is this constitutional order is succeeded by something better, or something worse, we will be asked whether we tried.

Notes

Introduction
Christopher Wolfe

1. See, for example, http://en.wikipedia.org/wiki/Jesusland_map.

2. See Christopher Wolfe, *Natural Law Liberalism* (New York: Cambridge University Press, 2006), chapter 1.

3. Amy Guttmann, *Democratic Education*, rev. ed. (Princeton: Princeton University Press, 1999).

4. James Dwyer, *Religious Schools v. Children's Rights*, (Ithaca, NY: Cornell University Press, 2001).

5. Stephen Macedo, *Diversity and Distrust* (Cambridge: Harvard University Press, 2000).

1. The Public Square: Naked No More?
Gerard V. Bradley

1. I would like to thank the organizers of the conference in which an earlier version of this paper was given: "How Naked a Public Square?: Reconsidering the Place of Religion in American Public Life," cosponsored by the James Madison Program in American Ideals and Institutions (Princeton University), the Center for Religious Inquiry Across the Disciplines (Baylor University), and the American Public Philosophy Institute; my special thanks to Robert P. George, director of the James Madison Program. Philip Hamburger and Christopher Eisgruber provided invaluable responses at the conference. Christopher Wolfe and Rick Garnett read this revised manuscript and each offered useful criticisms and suggestions for improvement.

2. Starting in 1947, the Court took a short detour in church-state consti-

tutional law, advancing a novel and highly secularized interpretation of the Establishment Clause in *Everson v. Board of Education*, 330 U.S. 1 (1947). This bold interpretation was confirmed the next year in *McCollum v. Board of Education*, 333 U.S. 203. In 1952, the Court returned to the mainstream of tradition. See *Zorach v. Clausen*, 343 U.S. 306 (1952). See generally Gerard Bradley, "The Judicial Experiment with Privatizing Religion," *Liberty Law Review* 1 (2006): 17.

3. *Engel*, 370 U.S. 421 (1962).
4. *Abington School District v. Schempp*, 374 U.S. 203 (1963).
5. *Schempp*, 374 U.S. at 213.
6. *Rosenberger v. Board of Visitors*, 515 U.S. 819, 861 (1995) (Thomas, J., concurring).
7. *Elk Grove Unified School District v. Newdow*, 542 U.S. 1, 45, n. 1 (2004) (Thomas, J., concurring).
8. *Allegheny*, 492 U.S. 573 (1989).
9. *Newdow*, 542 U.S. at 45, n. 1.
10. *Caldor*, 472 U.S. 703 (1985).
11. *Sherbert*, 374 U.S. 398 (1963).
12. *Oregon v. Smith*, 494 U.S. 872 (1990).
13. *Caldor*, 472 U.S. at 710.
14. Ibid., at n. 9.
15. Ibid.
16. *Jaffree*, 472 U.S. 38 (1985).
17. Ibid., at 59.
18. Ibid., at 59, n. 47.
19. *Aguilar*, 473 U.S. 402 (1985).
20. *Grand Rapids*, 473 U.S. 373 (1985).
21. *Ibid.*, 473 U.S. 387, 390–92.
22. *Employment Division, Dept. of Human Resources of Oregon v. Smith*, 494 U.S. 872 (1990).
23. See Gerard Bradley, "Beguiled: Free Exercise Conduct Exemptions and the Siren Song of Liberalism," *Hofstra Law Review* 20 (1991): 245.
24. *Cutter v. Wilkinson*, 544 U.S. 709 (2005).
25. Ibid., at 2123.
26. Ibid., at 2124.
27. *Agostini*, 521 U.S. 203 (1997).
28. See, e.g., *Mitchell v. Helms*, 530 U.S. 793 (2000).
29. *Zelman v. Simmons-Harris*, 536 U.S. 639 (2002).
30. *Lamb's Chapel v. Center Moriches Union Free School District*, 508 U.S. 384 (1993).

31. This is basically the result in *Lamb's Chapel*.

32. Essentially the result in *Rosenberger v. Rector and Board of Visitors of University of Virginia*, 515 U.S. 819 (1995).

33. See Bradley, supra n. 23, at 307–19.

34. The result in *Cutter* is much less ambiguous. But the reasoning in that case strains to the point of incoherence to *avoid* a flat-footed declaration in favor of religion over nonreligion.

35. See part III of this essay.

36. Transcript of Oral Argument at 11, *Engel v. Vitale*, 370 U.S. 421 (1962) (No. 468).

37. Ibid., at 26.

38. Ibid., at 28.

39. Ibid., at 42.

40. Ibid., at 14–15.

41. *Engel*, 370 U.S. at 430.

42. Ibid., at 435.

43. Ibid., at 432 (quoting James Madison's *Memorial and Remonstrance Against Religious Assessments* [1785]).

44. Ibid., at 445.

45. Ibid., at 450.

46. *Zorach*, 343 U.S. 306, 313 (1952).

47. *Newdow*, 542 U.S. 1 (2004).

48. Ibid., at 51.

49. See Robert P. George and William C. Porth, "Trimming the Ivy: A Bicentennial Re-examination of the Establishment Clause," *West Virginia Law Review* 90 (1987): 109. See also Vincent Munoz's article "The Original Meaning of the Establishment Clause and the Impossibility of its Incorporation," *University of Pennsylvania Constitutional Law Review*, Vol. 8 (2006).

50. Justice Scalia did not participate in *Newdow*.

51. For a scholarly argument see Gerard Bradley, *Church-State Relationships in America* (New York: Greenwood Press, 1987). Justices Scalia and Thomas adopted the sect-equality reading in the *Lamb's Chapel* case.

52. *Newdow*, 542 U.S. at 40 (O'Connor, J., concurring).

53. Ibid., at 31.

54. Ibid.

55. Ibid.

56. Ibid.

57. Ibid., at 40.

58. Ibid.

59. Ibid., at 35.
60. Ibid., at 36.
61. Ibid., at 35.
62. Ibid., at 36.
63. Ibid.
64. Ibid., at 37.
65. Ibid.
66. Ibid., at 36.
67. Ibid.
68. Ibid., at 43.
69. Ibid., at 34.
70. R. Laurence Moore, *Religious Outsiders and the Making of Americans* (New York: Oxford University Press, 1986), xi.
71. Ibid.
72. *Newdow*, 542 U.S. at 48 (Thomas, J., concurring).
73. Statement of L. Rabaut, Pledge of Allegiance: Hearing on H. J. Res. 243 before the House Subcommittee No. 5 (Judiciary), 83rd Cong. 7–8 (1954) (unpublished hearing microprint on CIS No. 83 HJ-T-75 [Congressional Information Service]).
74. Ibid., 33.
75. Ibid., 7.
76. Ibid., 11.
77. U.S. Code Congressional and Administrative News, 83rd Cong., 2nd Sess. 1954, Vol. 2, 2340.
78. Hearings before the Committee on Banking and Currency, HR 84th Cong., 1st Sess. on H.J. Res. 202, May 17, 1955, 49.
79. Ibid.
80. Ibid., at 51. Bennett also testified that he knew of "no opposition to this legislation." Congressman Multer of Illinois voiced a reservation, however, about so promiscuously mixing mammon with God: "I don't believe it has inspired one single person to be more religious because we have those words on our currency." Ibid., at 50. Nonetheless Multer concluded: "I would not oppose the bill." Ibid. Congressman Eberharter of Pennsylvania thought the greenback might do more than did Radio Free Europe: "[T]he American dollar travels all over the world, into every country of the world, and frequently gets behind the Iron Curtain, and if it carries this message in that way I think it would be very good." Ibid., at 53.
81. The focus in the text is on civil religion from above: political leaders' attempts to harness the energy and ideas of religion to state purposes.

But civil religion from below is just as common. Here is an example, an excerpt from a speech on the Communist threat, delivered by Francis Cardinal Spellman, Archbishop of New York, to the Knights of Columbus in August 1950: "[T]o live, to love, if need be to fight and die for God's glory, our country, and our brother, should be the self-command of every American citizen and patriot, as, with avowed allegiance to his faith, his flag, and his fellowman, he aspires to become the inspiration of his own generation and the salvation of generations of Americans yet unborn." Quoted in Joshua M. Zeitz, *White Ethnic New York* (Raleigh, NC: University of North Carolina Press, 2007), 88.

82. See Bradley, *Church-State Relationships in America*.

83. *Watson*, 80 U.S. 679, 728 (1871).

84. *Newdow*, at 42, quoting Scalia, J., dissenting in *Lee v. Weisman*, 505 U.S. at 641.

85. *Newdow*, at 42, scare quotes in original.

86. Ibid.

87. 542 U.S. at 42.

2. The Naked Public Square Today: A Secular Public Square?

Mary Ann Glendon

1. Richard John Neuhaus, *The Naked Public Square*: *Religion and Democracy in America* (Grand Rapids: William B. Eerdmans Publishing Co., 1984): 125.

2. The trend is exemplified by the series of cases where the Court has sustained efforts to ban religious expression in public school settings. See, e.g., *Wallace v. Jaffree*, 472 U.S. 38 (1985) (moment of silence); *Lee v. Weisman*, 505 U.S. 577 (1992) (prayer at graduation ceremony); *Santa Fe Indep. School Dist. v. Doe*, 530 U.S. 290 (2000) (student-led, student-initiated prayer before football games); see also *Locke v. Davey*, 540 U.S. 712 (2004) (ruling that a publicly funded scholarship program may exclude the study of theology); *Employment Div. v. Smith*, 494 U.S. 872 (1990) (holding that religious individuals were not constitutionally entitled to exemptions from statutes of general applicability); but see *Corporation of the Presiding Bishop v. Amos*, 483 U.S. 327 (1987) (upholding unanimously the statutory religious exemption to the employment discrimination sections of the Civil Rights Act); *Bowen v. Kendrick*, 487 U.S. 589 (1988) (allowing federal funding for religious pregnancy counseling and thus providing a basis for further experiments with faith-based

charity initiatives); and *Zelman v. Simmons-Harris*, 536 U.S. 639 (2002) (upholding the use of school vouchers for religious schools).

3. See, e.g., Robert L. Cord, *Separation of Church and State: Historical Fact and Current Fiction* (New York: Lambeth Press, 1982); Mark DeWolfe Howe, *The Garden and the Wilderness* (Chicago: University of Chicago Press, 1965); Philip E. Johnson, "Concepts and Compromise in First Amendment Religious Doctrine," *California Law Review* 72 (1984): 817; John H. Mansfield, "The Religion Clauses of the First Amendment and the Philosophy of the Constitution," *California Law Review* 72 (1984): 847–48 ("[M]ost will agree that there is a need for a more encompassing and clearer view both of the religion clauses of the first amendment and also of the relation between the religion clauses and other provisions of the Constitution. . . . [A] tendency on the part of the Court and commentators to see cases as either Free Exercise Clause cases or Establishment Clause cases has impeded true understanding. It is necessary to see the religion clauses as working together to create a single standard that dictates the proper relation between government and religion."); Jesse H. Choper, "The Religion Clauses of the First Amendment: Reconciling the Conflict," *University of Pittsburgh Law Review* 41 (1980): 673–75; Philip B. Kurland, "The Irrelevance of the Constitution: The Religion Clauses of the First Amendment and the Supreme Court," *Villanova Law Review* 24 (1979): 3, 24 (stating that "the Constitution has been essentially irrelevant to the judgments of the United States Supreme Court in the areas designated freedom of religion and separation of church and state. . . . [T]he religion clauses were not separate mandates but a single one. . . ."); Wilber G. Katz, "Radiations from Church Tax Exemption," *Supreme Court Review* (1970): 93–94 ("[I]n the interpretation of both clauses the Court's responsibility . . . is 'to do loyal service . . . to the ultimate First Amendment objective of religious liberty'" (internal citation omitted)).

4. Richard John Neuhaus, "A New Order of Religious Freedom," *First Things* (February 1992): 13–17. See also Mary Ann Glendon and Raul F. Yanes, "Structural Free Exercise," *Michigan Law Review* 90 (1991): 541.

5. See, e.g., *Lynch v. Donnelly*, 465 U.S. 668, 688 (1984) (O'Connor, J., concurring) (suggesting that Establishment Clause analysis should consider broadly whether the government is endorsing religion); *County of Allegheny v. ACLU*, 492 U.S. 573 (1989) (a majority of the court adopting Justice O'Connor's endorsement test); *Wallace v. Jaffree*, 472 U.S. 38 (1985) (holding that one minute per day of silent prayer or meditation in public school violates the Establishment Clause); *Lee v. Weisman*, 505 U.S. 577 (1992) (holding unconstitutional nonsectarian prayer at a public school graduation by a clergyman selected by the school).

6. See, e.g., *Goldman v. Weinberger*, 475 U.S. 503 (1986) (denying Jewish Air Force officer the right to wear a yarmulke while in uniform); *Employment Division v. Smith*, 494 U.S. 872 (1990) (denying exemption for sacramental peyote use).

7. *Locke v. Davey*, 540 U.S. 712 (2004).

8. See, e.g., *Bush v. Holmes*, 29 *Florida Law Weekly* D 1877 (Florida District Court App. 2004) (citing *Locke v. Davey* as permitting judicial invalidation of the Florida Opportunity Scholarship Program, under a state constitutional provision requiring that "[n]o revenue of the state . . . shall ever be taken from the public treasury directly or indirectly in aid of any church, sect, or religious denomination or in aid of any sectarian institution," because the program's tuition vouchers could be used at religious schools); see generally Douglas Laycock, "Theology Scholarships, the Pledge of Allegiance, and Religious Liberty: Avoiding the Extremes but Missing the Liberty," *Harvard Law Review* 118 (2004) (construing *Locke v. Davey* as permitting significant religious discrimination in funding cases).

9. Peter Berger and Richard John Neuhaus, *To Empower People: The Role of Mediating Structures in Public Policy* (Washington, D.C.: AEI Press, 1977), 3.

10. See, e.g., Exec. Order No. 13, 199, *Establishment of White House Office of Faith-Based and Community Initiatives*, 66 Fed. Reg. 8499 (Jan. 29, 2001), available online at http://www.whitehouse.gov/news/releases/2001/01/20010129–2.html; Exec. Order No. 13,198, *Agency Responsibilities with Respect to Faith-Based and Community Initiatives*, 66 Fed. Reg. 8497 (Jan. 29, 2001), available online at http://www.whitehouse.gov/news/releases/2001/01/20010129–3.html.

11. See *Catholic Charities of Sacramento v. Superior Court*, 85 P.3d 67 (Cal. 2004), *cert. denied* 543 U.S.—(docket no. 03–1618) (Oct. 4, 2004). The court found that Catholic Charities did not meet any of the four required statutory elements defining a religious employer: a primary purpose of inculcating religious values; primary employment of people who share the employer's religious values; primary service toward people who share the employer's religious values; and recognition under the tax code as a church, church auxiliary, church association, or exclusively religious activity of a religious order. A nearly identical case is currently on appeal within the New York state courts. A nearly identical case is *Catholic Charities of the Diocese of Albany, et al. v. Serio*, 859 N.E. 2d 459 (NYCA 2006).

12. See 6 Admin. Code NYC §6–126; see also David Andreatta, "Council Overrides Bloomberg's Veto on Gay Benefits," *New York Sun*, June 29,

2004; Brad Hamilton, "'Army' Girds for Gay War," *The New York Post*, May 23, 2004.

13. See, e.g., *Good News Club v. Milford Cent. Sch.*, 533 U.S. 98 (2001) (allowing a religious club to meet at school facilities during nonschool hours); *Westside Board of Education v. Mergens*, 496 U.S. 226 (1990) (upholding the Equal Access Act, mandating that noncurricular clubs be allowed equal access to facilities irrespective of their religious nature).

14. See, e.g., *Abington School District v. Schempp*, 374 U.S. 203 (1963) (banning school-sponsored prayer and scripture reading even with allowance for student opt-out); *Stone v. Graham*, 449 U.S. 39 (1980) (disallowing the posting of the Ten Commandments in classrooms); *Wallace v. Jaffree*, 472 U.S. 38 (1985) (disallowing a state law allowing silence for meditation or prayer at the beginning of class because of perceived religious motivation for the law); *County of Allegheny v. ACLU*, 492 U.S. 573 (1989) (disallowing display of religious symbols on public property); *Lee v. Weisman*, 505 U.S. 577 (1992) (disallowing graduation prayers by clergy); *Santa Fe Indep. School District v. Doe*, 530 U.S. 290 (2000) (disallowing student prayers at high school football games); *Locke v. Davey*, 540 U.S. 712 (2004) (allowing a public scholarship fund to exclude solely theology majors, thereby paving the way to exclude religious schools from voucher programs; see supra n. 8).

15. *Wisconsin v. Yoder*, 406 U.S. 205, 232 (1972); see also *Troxel v. Granville*, 530 U.S. 57, 65–66 (2000) (recognizing that the right of parents "to control the education of their children" "is perhaps the oldest of the fundamental liberty interests recognized by this Court"); *Pierce v. Society of Sisters*, 268 U.S. 510, 534–35 (1925) (recognizing "the liberty of parents and guardians to direct the upbringing and education of [their] children"); *Meyer v. Nebraska*, 262 U.S. 390, 401 (1923) (invalidating a state law because it interfered with "the power of parents to control the education of their own").

16. Stephen Carter, "Liberalism's Religion Problem," *First Things* (March 2002): 21–32.

17. *Zelman v. Simmons-Harris*, 536 U.S. 639 (2002).

18. See, e.g., *Bush v. Holmes*, 29 *Florida Law Weekly* D 1877 (Florida District Court App. 2004) (invalidating the Florida Opportunity Scholarship Program because the program's tuition vouchers could be used at religious schools); see generally Mark Edward DeForrest, "An Overview and Evaluation of State Blaine Amendments: Origins, Scope, and First Amendment Concerns," *Harvard Journal of Law & Public Policy* 26 (2003): 551.

19. See Michael W. McConnell, "Why Is Religious Liberty the 'First Freedom'?," *Cardozo Law Review* 21 (2000): 1263–64; Michael W. McCon-

nell, "Governments, Families, and Power: A Defense of Educational Choice," *Connecticut Law Review* 31 (1999): 849–52; see also Stephen Smith, "The Pluralist Predicament," *Legal Theory* 10 (2004): 60–75.

20. Smith, "The Pluralist Predicament," 68.

21. John Stuart Mill, *On Liberty*, (Indianapolis: Bobbs-Merrill, 1956), 22, ch. 5.

22. See, for example, Stephen Macedo's suggestion that a liberal democratic government should discourage those religions that are most assertively nonliberal. Stephen Macedo, "Transformative Constitutionalism and the Case of Religion: Defending the Moderate Hegemony of Liberalism," *Political Theory* 26 (1988): 61–63.

23. Michael Novak, "Truth and Liberty: The Present Crisis in our Culture," *Review of Politics* 59 (1997): 8.

24. Madison, *Federalist* 55, ed. Rossiter (New York: New American Library, 1961), 344.

25. Neuhaus, *The Naked Public Square*, 84.

26. William A. Galston, *Liberal Purposes: Goods, Virtues, and Diversity in the Liberal State* (New York: Cambridge University Press, 1991), 6.

27. Neuhaus, *The Naked Public Square*, 140.

3. The Naked European Constitution
J. H. H. Weiler

1. This did not include books dealing with specific aspects such as agriculture or competition. In the exceptional cases when Christianity was mentioned, it was usually in the context of subsidiarity, which, though sharing the same name with the famous Christian social doctrine, has, in the hands of most, little else in common.

4. Religion in a Liberal Democracy: Foundation or Threat?
Michael Pakaluk

1. Iain T. Benson, "Notes Towards a (Re) Definition of the 'Secular'," *University of British Columbia Law Review*, Special Issue (2000), "Religion, Morality and Law," 33:519–49.

2. Robert P. George, The Clash of Orthodoxies (Wilmington, DE: ISI Books, 2001), 18–19.

3. Ibid., 19.

4. Ibid., 4.

5. Avery Cardinal Dulles, "The Deist Minimum," *First Things* (January, 2005), 149:25–30.

6. Mark C. Henrie, "Rethinking American Conservatism in the 1990s: The Struggle against Homogenization," *Intercollegiate Review* 28:2 (Spring 1993) 8–16; Robert Nisbet, *Conservatism: Dream and Reality* (Minneapolis: University of Minnesota Press, 1986).

7. George Marsden, "God and Man at Yale (1880)," *First Things* (April, 1994), 42:39.

8. The limits to accuracy in social and political philosophy, which Aristotle commented upon (in *Nicomachean Ethics* 1.4) are limits too, upon what kind of principle we can in practice remember, rely upon, and make use of in ordinary life.

9. Charles Taylor, "The Diversity of Goods," in Amartya Sen and Bernard Williams, eds., *Utilitarianism and Beyond* (Cambridge: Cambridge University Press, 1982), 129–44.

10. Peter Singer, "All Animals are Equal," in Tom Regan and Peter Singer, eds., *Animal Rights and Human Obligations*, 2nd ed. (Englewood Cliffs: Prentice Hall, 1989), 148–62.

11. Michael Tooley, "Abortion and Infanticide," *Philosophy and Public Affairs*, 2:1 (Fall 1972), 37–65.

12. John Rawls, *Political Liberalism* (New York: Columbia University Press, 1993), 243, n. 32.

13. Ibid., paperback edition (1995), 231–40.

14. *The Lincoln-Douglas Debates*, Harold Holzer, ed. (New York: Fordham University Press, 2004), 350.

15. 2002 SCC 86.

5. Telling the Truth about God and Man in a Pluralist Society: Economy or Explication?
John Finnis

1. For Newman's thoughts on this economy, which like the tradition's draw upon several of the senses of the Greek term *oeconomia* and appeal to telling scriptural sayings (no pearls before swine, no crushing the bruised reed, the tares left among the wheat) and examples (Paul's address to the Areopagus in Athens: *Acts* 17:22–31), see his *Fifteen Sermons Preached before the University of Oxford* ([1843], 3rd ed. 1871, 1909), 341–50; *Apologia Pro Vita Sua* ([1864, 1865], combined ed. 1913), 45–46, 270, 343–46; *The Arians of the Fourth Century* ([1833], 1871), 65–77.

2. John Finnis, *Aquinas: Moral, Political, and Legal Theory* (New York: Oxford University Press, 1998), 305.

3. "And so it is clear that the natural law is precisely the sharing out of the

eternal law in the rational creature [*participatio legis aeternae in rationali creatura*]": *Summa Theologiae* I–II q. 91 a. 2c. It is *as* the natural law in this sense that the eternal law is the standard for human willing [*regula voluntatis humanae*]: I–II q. 71 a. 6c.

4. Plato attributes much the same importance to achieving likeness with God: see *Laws* 4. 716; *Republic* 6. 501. The ideal is the more attractive when put in the frame of Christian revelation's disclosure of God as intelligent, free, self-possessed, and generous, as well as (to use the predicate that Plato picks out as central) moderate. See Finnis, *Aquinas*, 314–15.

5. See Finnis, *Aquinas*, 99–100.

6. Ibid., 308–9.

7. On the legitimate secularism which is part of Christian doctrine, see, e.g., Finnis, *Aquinas*, 322–25; John Finnis, "On the Practical Meaning of Secularism," *Notre Dame Law Review* 73 (1998): 491.

8. *Psalm* 19:1; and see *Romans* 1:19–20ff, which opens up into the Pauline account of natural law: 2:14–16.

9. For this use of "mark" (a term much used by Newman), see the summary and discussion of David Wiggins's account of truth, in John Finnis, *Fundamentals of Ethics* (New York: Oxford University Press and Georgetown University Press, 1983), 63–66.

10. John Finnis, Joseph Boyle, and Germain Grisez, *Nuclear Deterrence, Morality, and Realism* (New York: Oxford University Press, 1987), 38–44.

11. *Nicomachean Ethics*, 1.4: 1095b4–8.

12. Finnis, *Aquinas*, 320–21, citing *Summa Theologiae* III q. 40 a. 1c and ad 4, q. 42 a. 1 ad 2, a. 4c.

13. See Rawls, *Political Liberalism* ([1993], New York: Columbia University Press, 1996), 45, where Rawls expounds the idea without the phrase put into currency by his *A Theory of Justice*.

14. See Vatican Council II, Dogmatic Constitution on Divine Revelation, *Dei Verbum*, 8.2: " . . . *crescit enim tam rerum quam verborum traditorum perceptio, tum ex contemplatione et studio credentium, qui ea conferunt in corde suo . . . , tum ex intima spiritualium rerum quam experiuntur intelligentia . . . Ecclesia scilicet, volventibus saeculis, ad plenitudinem divinae veritatis iugiter tendit . . .* ": "For insight into the realities and words handed down grows, through the reflection and study of the faithful who ponder these things in their hearts, and through the penetrating understanding of the spiritual realities of which they have experience. . . . Thus, over the centuries, the Church is constantly heading towards the fullness of divine truth . . ." [I have quoted economically]. On development of

doctrine through differentiation, see, e.g., John Finnis, *Moral Absolutes* (Washington, D.C.: CUA Press, 1991), 25–27.

15. This should not be translated as "of human dignity," since the document's first three words are *"Dignitatis humanae personae,"* and in the context of the whole sentence, the adjective *humanae* qualifies *personae*, not *dignitatis*.

16. See Finnis, *Aquinas*, 222–28.

17. *Dignitatis Humanae*, sec. 3.4

18. Ibid., sec. 10.

19. Ibid., secs. 10, 12.1. For critical observations on the coercion that from the fourth to the eighteenth century was often applied, with ecclesiastical and theological approval, against those who *departed* from the Catholic faith (as distinct from pagans, Jews, Muslims, etc.), see Finnis, *Aquinas*, 292. The unbelief of pagans, etc. was judged harmful to the common good (*Summa Theologiae* II–II q. 10 aa. 7c & 10c) but not culpable like heresy, which was (mis)conceived of as a breach of promise and met with punishment; the thesis that these positions and measures were distinguishable from compulsion of belief (a compulsion always rejected: see II–II q. 12 a. 2c & ad 2; *Scriptum super Libros Sententiarum* IV d. 13 q.2 a. 3 ad 5) was inherently unsound.

20. *Dignitatis Humanae* does not mention the concept of being "made in God's image," but was adopted and promulgated simultaneously with the much more expansive document *Gaudium et Spes*, the Pastoral Constitution on the Church in the Modern World, which devotes sections 12 to 22 to "The Dignity of the Human Person," and begins sec. 12 with the heading *De homine in imaginem Dei*: on the human being as made in the image of God.

21. Writing of Charles Larmore's (and, he might have added, Ronald Dworkin's) notion that equality of respect for persons requires state neutrality about the good life, Kent Greenawalt pertinently says: "Although many defenses of equality rely on moral capacity, it remains unclear why people should be owed equal respect based on a capacity *if* the capacity itself is unequal among people and is exercised to unequal degrees. The problem is *resolved* by some comprehensive views, most notably by the religious idea that all human beings are equally loved by God and are equal in God's sight, but it seems doubtful if the basic principle of equal respect can be grounded without reference to some comprehensive view." Kent Greenawalt, *Private Consciences and Public Reasons* (New York: Oxford University Press, 1995), 82.

22. In its discussion of atheism in *Gaudium et Spes* 19–21, at 21, Vatican II

states (rightly, I think) that acknowledging God in no way diminishes human dignity, a dignity grounded and brought to perfection in God, and that when people are deprived of divine support (of hope in life to come, and knowledge that one has been placed in the world by God, who created us as intelligent and free beings) "their dignity is deeply impaired, as may so often be seen today." The whole of this section repays study, not least its condemnation of discrimination by civil authorities between believers and unbelievers, and its invitation to unbelievers to weigh the merits of Christ's Gospel with an open mind.

23. See Finnis, *Aquinas*, 297.

24. On the synonymity (in his articulation of the criterion for reasons being public) of "endorse" and "affirm" and "agree," see Rawls, *Political Liberalism*, 39, 241.

25. See, e.g., Jean Hampton, "The Moral Commitments of Liberalism," in David Copp, Jean Hampton, and John E. Roemer, *The Idea of Democracy* (New York: Cambridge University Press, 1993), 292–313; John Finnis, "Practical Reason, Abortion and Cloning," *Valparaiso University Law Review* 32 (1998): 361–83.

26. On the ambiguity of "can *be expected* to" (or "can reasonably *be expected* to"), see Finnis, "Practical Reason, Abortion, and Cloning," at 365–66.

27. Rawls, *Political Liberalism*, lvi nn. 31, 32; 244 n. 32.

28. Ibid., 152–53.

29. Cf., e.g., ibid., lv: "if when stand-offs occur, citizens invoke the grounding reasons of their comprehensive view [as they do when they discount the rationalist believer's ideas: JMF], then the principle of reciprocity is violated." In the same passage (in the Introduction to the Paperback Edition, lvi n. 31), Rawls says that on questions like abortion, he doesn't know whether there are any "most reasonable or decisive" arguments (within the domain of public reason). He continues to avoid confronting the question why it is outside public reason to argue from the premise that human rights belong equally to all human beings/persons, and the premise that unborn children are human beings/persons (as is obvious whenever the baby is wanted), to the conclusion that unborn babies have the equal right to life. In 1993, he seemed committed (ibid., 243) to regarding such an argument as paradigmatically unreasonable; in 1996, he seemed to regard it as perhaps reasonable or perhaps unreasonable but in any case capable of being either held or rejected by reasonable people, and to be decided in practice by voting. To me it seems reasonable, and his own position paradigmatically unreasonable. (*N.B.*, the issue as he sets it up concerns not obstetrical emergencies but the unborn dur-

ing early pregnancy and the overriding of their life by concerns such as "equality of women" (with men) (243n).

30. Abdullah Saeed (Professor of Arab & Islamic Studies in the University of Melbourne) and Hassan Saeed (Attorney General of the Maldives), *Freedom of Religion, Apostasy, and Islam* (Aldershot, Hants, England; Burlington, VT: Ashgate, 2004) argue, in relation to Malaysia (chosen because it is one of the most moderate Muslim-majority states) that capital punishment for apostasy is not warranted by the Quran. They note that "there does appear to be general consensus within the Malaysian Muslim community that some form of action ought to be taken to check the growing influence of Christianity in the region" (164), and predict that legal penalties ("coated with euphemisms such as 'rehabilitation' and 'education'") for apostasy from Islam are likely to continue, despite their incompatibility with the constitution adopted at the end of British rule. Their final word is that, throughout the Muslim world, "only a few are arguing for doing away with apostasy laws that adversely affect the individual's basic rights as a person.")

31. In reflecting on the outcome of a free discourse about Islam and Catholic Christianity, recall that its core is necessarily a comparison between (the moral characters of) Muhammad and Jesus: see text and n. 12. And see Aquinas, *Summa contra Gentiles* I, c. 6 n. 7.

32. The Bible is the Catholic Church's book and confirms its teachings, but for many centuries the Church's leaders predicted that if it were generally available to everyone in their own languages, it would be extensively misunderstood and turned against the very doctrines that, understood as a whole, it fully supports. The prediction has been very amply fulfilled over the centuries since 1500. But it would be a mistake to infer that people do not have the right of access to all the materials of public revelation and equally a mistake to predict that in the long run, the result of giving effect to that right will be to defeat the Church's evangelical mission.

33. Joseph Butler, who preceded Newman at Oriel College Oxford by about a century and who influenced his philosophical theology, prefaced his *Analogy of Religion Natural and Revealed to the Constitution and Course of Nature* (1736) with the observation: "It is come, I know not how, to be taken for granted, by many persons, that Christianity is not so much as a subject of inquiry; but that it is now, at length, discovered to be fictitious. And accordingly, they treat it as if, in the present age, this were *an agreed point among all people of discernment*; and nothing remained, but to set it up as a principal subject of mirth and ridicule, as it were by way of reprisals, for its having so long interrupted the pleasures of the world"

(emphasis added). Predictions made by elite intellectuals in 1735 about the likely condition of Christianity two and a half centuries later would very probably have been wide of the mark.

34. Note that "any action which seems to suggest coercion or dishonest or unworthy persuasion, especially when one is dealing with the uneducated or poor, . . . must be considered . . . an infringement of the rights of others": *Dignitatis Humanae* 4.4.

6. Revelation and Democratic Responsibilities: A Comment on Finnis

Rogers M. Smith

1. John Rawls, *The Law of Peoples: with "The Idea of Public Reason Revisited"* (Cambridge: Harvard University Press, 1999).

2. John Locke, *A Letter Concerning Toleration*, ed. James Tully, (Indianapolis: Hackett Publishing Company, 1983). See also Rogers M. Smith, *Stories of Peoplehood: The Politics and Morals of Political Membership* (New York: Cambridge University Press, 2003).

3. Smith, *Stories of Peoplehood*, 154–74.

4. See, for example, Michael McConnell, "The Origins and Historical Understanding of Free Exercise of Religion," *Harvard Law Review* Vol. 103 (1990) 1409–98, and "Equal Treatment and Religious Discrimination" in *Equal Treatment of Religion in a Pluralistic Society*, ed. Stephen V. Monsma and J. Christopher Soper (Grand Rapids: William B. Eerdmans Publishing Co., 1998) 30–54.

5. Rogers M. Smith, "'Equal' Treatment? A Liberal Separationist View," in Monsma and Soper, eds., *Equal Treatment of Religion in a Pluralistic Society*, 179–99.

6. Robert P. George, "Introduction: Protecting Religious Liberty in the Next Millennium: Should We Amend the Religion Clauses of the Constitution?" *Loyola of Los Angeles Law Review*, Vol. 32 (1998), 27–49.

7. For example, *Abington School District v. Schempp,* 374 U.S. 203 (1963).

8. *McGowan v. Maryland,* 366 U.S. 420 (1961).

9. George W. Bush, "Inaugural Address," January 20, 2001, at http://www.presidency.ucsb.edu, accessed February 20, 2009, by entering date and category of speech.

10. George W. Bush, "Address to Joint Session of Congress and the American People," September 20, 2001, at http://www.presidency.ucsb.edu, accessed February 20, 2009 by entering date and category of speech.

11. Caryn D. Riswold, "A Religious Response Veiled in a Presidential

Address: A Theological Study of Bush's Speech on 20 September 2001," *Political Theology*, Vol. 5 (2004), 44–46.

12. On this point, I draw on my essay "Religious Rhetoric and Ethics of Political Discourse: The Case of George W. Bush," *Political Theory* 36:279–87, which relies in part on Coe and Domke, "Petitioners or Prophets? Presidential Discourse, God, and the Ascendancy of Religious Conservatives," *Journal of Communications* 56 (2006): 309–30.

13. George W. Bush, "1st State of the Union Address," January 29, 2002, at http://www.presidency.ucsb.edu, accessed February 20, 2009, by entering date and category of speech.

14. George W. Bush, "Remarks on September 11, 2002, at Ellis Island," at http://www.presidency.ucsb.edu, accessed February 20, 2009, by entering date and category of speech.

15. George W. Bush, "2nd State of the Union Address," January 23, 2003, at http://www.presidency.ucsb.edu, accessed February 20, 2009, by entering date and category of speech.

16. George W. Bush, "Remarks on the 20th Anniversary of the National Endowment for Democracy," November 6, 2003 at http://www.presidency.ucsb.edu, accessed February 20, 2009, by entering date and category of speech.

17. George W. Bush, "3rd State of the Union Address," January 20, 2004, at http://www.presidency.ucsb.edu, accessed February 20, 2009, by entering date and category of speech.

18. George W. Bush, "2nd Nomination Acceptance Speech," September 2, 2004, at http://www.presidency.ucsb.edu, accessed February 20, 2009 by entering date and category of speech.

19. George W. Bush, "2nd Inaugural Address," January 20, 2005, at http://www.presidency.ucsb.edu, accessed February 20, 2009, by entering date and category of speech.

20. Abraham Lincoln, "2nd Inaugural Address," March 4, 1865, at http://www.presidency.ucsb.edu, accessed February 20, 2009, by entering date and category of speech.

21. George W. Bush, "4th State of the Union Address," February 2, 2005, at http://www.presidency.ucsb.edu, accessed February 20, 2009, by entering date and category of speech.

22. Judy Keen, "White House Staffers Gather for Bible Study," *USA Today*, October 13, 2002, available online at http://www.usatoday.com/news/washington/2003-10-13-bible-usat_x.htm.

23. George W. Bush, "National Day of Prayer Remarks," May 6, 2004, at http://www.presidency.ucsb.edu, accessed February 20, 2009, by entering date and category of speech.

7. Response to John Finnis:
Inviting More Explication and More Economy

Eric Gregory

1. Karl Barth, *Community, State, and Church* (Garden City: Doubleday, 1960).

2. My formulation borrows from Robert P. George, *Making Men Moral: Civil Liberties and Public Morality* (Oxford: Oxford University Press, 1993).

3. For discussion of these trends illustrated through the work of Stanley Hauerwas and John Milbank, see Jeffrey Stout, *Democracy and Tradition* (Princeton: Princeton University Press, 2004).

4. Richard John Neuhaus, *The Naked Public Square: Religion and Democracy in America*, (Grand Rapids: William B. Eerdmans Publishing Co., 1984), 66. For a compelling theological discussion of this theme, see John Finnis, Joseph Boyle, and Germain Grisez, *Nuclear Deterrence, Morality, and Realism* (Oxford: Oxford University Press, 1987). The authors claim that the "Church of Christ, not the West, is the true bearer of the hopes of ancient Israel" (375).

5. John Finnis, "Telling the Truth About God and Man in a Pluralistic Society: Economy or Explication?", supra, 115.

6. *Gaudium et Spes* (December 7, 1965): 4.76.

7. For a recent statement that effectively defends these kinds of claims, see Christopher Eberle, *Religious Conviction in Liberal Politics* (Cambridge: Cambridge University Press, 2002).

8. John Rawls, *Political Liberalism* (New York: Columbia University Press, 1996), 42–43. See also John Rawls, "The Idea of Public Reason Revisited," in Samuel Freeman, ed., *John Rawls: Collected Papers* (Cambridge: Harvard University Press, 1999), 574. For Rawls' early theological views on politics, see Eric Gregory, "Before the Original Position: The Neo-Orthodox Theology of the Young John Rawls," *Journal of Religious Ethics* 35:2 (June 2007), 179–206.

9. For diverse criticisms of Finnis on these matters, see Russell Hittinger, *A Critique of the New Natural Law Theory* (Notre Dame: University of Notre Dame Press, 1987); John Bowlin, *Contingency and Fortune in Aquinas's Ethics* (Cambridge: Cambridge University Press, 1999); and G. Scott Davis, "Doing What Comes Naturally: Recent Work on Aquinas and the New Natural Law Theory," *Religion* 31 (2001): 407–33.

10. Augustine, *On Christian Doctrine*, trans. D. W. Robertson, Jr., (Upper Saddle River, NJ: Prentice-Hall, 1958), I.XIII.

11. Finnis, "Telling the Truth," 109.

12. John Finnis, *Aquinas: Moral, Political, and Legal Theory* (Oxford: Oxford University Press, 1998), 320.

13. Ibid., 321.

14. Finnis, "Telling the Truth," 103.

15. Ibid., 228.

16. For elaboration of this view by a Protestant political theologian, see Oliver O'Donovan, *The Desire of the Nations* (Cambridge: Cambridge University Press, 1996).

17. Finnis, "Telling the Truth," 111.

18. Ibid., 113.

19. Ibid., 114.

20. Ibid., 114.

8. Religious Pluralism and the Limits of Public Reason

William A. Galston

1. Langdon Gilkey, "Social and Intellectual Sources on Contemporary Protestant Theology in America," *Daedalus* (Winter 1967): 72.

2. William G. McLoughlin, "Is There a Third Force in Christendom?" *Daedalus* (Winter 1967): 50–51.

3. Richard John Neuhaus, *The Naked Public Square: Religion and Democracy in America* (Grand Rapids: William B. Eerdmans Publishing Co., 1984), 19.

4. Ibid., 36.

5. Ibid., 36.

6. Ibid., 125.

7. See William A. Galston, *The Practice of Liberal Pluralism* (New York: Cambridge University Press, 2004), chapter 4.

8. Neuhaus, *Naked Public Square*, 111.

9. For the classical distinction between (rational) divine ordinances and (unfathomable) edicts, see the Babylonian Talmud, Yoma 67b. For Miamonides' discussion, which qualifies but does not erase this distinction, see *The Guide of the Perplexed* 3:31, 26–27.

10. Julian (Yeol) Jakobovits, "Cloning and Its Challenges," *The Torah U-Madda Journal* 9 (2000): 195.

11. Union of Orthodox Jewish Congregations of America and the Rabbinical Council of America, "Cloning Research, Jewish Tradition & Public Policy," April, 2002. Available online at http://www.ou.org/public/Publib/cloninglet.htm.

12. Babylonian Talmud, Tractate Baba mezi'a 59b.

13. Avraham Steingbert, "Human Cloning—Scientific, Moral, and Jewish Perspectives," *The Torah U-Madda Journal* 9 (2000): 202.

14. Kenneth Waxman, "Creativity and Catharsis: A Theological Framework for Evaluating Cloning," *The Torah U-Madda Journal* 9 (2000): 191.

15. See Breitowitz, "The Preembryo in Halacha," available online at http://www.jlaw.com/Articles/preemb.html.

16. Ibid., 5.

17. Ibid., 7.

18. Quoted in Daniel Eisenberg, "Stem Cell Research in Jewish Law," available online at http://www.jlaw.com/Articles/stemcellres.html.

19. Quoted in Eisenberg, "Stem Cell Research in Jewish Law," 9.

20. Ibid., 13, fn. 49.

21. Moshe Dovid Tendler, "Stem Cell Research and Therapy: A Judeo-Biblical Perspective," *Ethical Issues in Human Stem Cell Research, Volume III*: *Religious Perspectives* (Rockville, MD: National Bioethics Advisory Commission, 2000), H-4.

22. Rabbi Michael J. Broyde, "Artificial Intelligence: A Complete—and we mean complete—Halachic Guide to Cloning." Manuscript on file with author.

23. Broyde, "Artificial Intelligence," 13–14.

24. Barry Freundel, "Judaism," in J. Robert Nelson, ed., *On the New Frontiers of Genetics and Religion* (Grand Rapids: William B. Eerdmans Publishing Co., 1994).

25. Quoted in Broyde, "Artificial Intelligence," 16, fn. 18.

26. "Statement of Professor Wilson" in *Human Cloning and Human Dignity*: *The Report of the President's Council on Bioethics* (New York: Public Affairs, 2002), 348–49.

27. For the quotation, original source, and discussion, see Feige Kaplan, "Human and Molecular Cloning: Ethical Dilemmas in a Brave New World," *The Torah U-Madda Journal* 9 (2000): 227.

9. Looking Back from 2034:
The Naked Public Square—Fifty Years Later
Hadley Arkes

1. "The Farmer Refuted," [February 1775], in *The Papers of Alexander Hamilton*, ed. Harold C. Syrett (New York: Columbia University Press, 1961), 1:86–87.

2. McLean in *Dred Scott v. Sanford*, 19 Howard 393, at 550 (1857).

3. Henry James, "The Solution" in *Complete Stories 1884–1891* (New York: Library of America, 1999).
4. *The Collected Works of Abraham Lincoln,* ed. Roy P. Basler (New Brunswick, NJ: Rutgers University Press, 1953), 3: 417 (Speeches in Columbus and Cincinnati, Ohio, September 16, 17, 1858).
5. Ibid., 549 (Speech at Cooper Union, February 27, 1860).
6. *Bob Jones University v. U.S.* 461 U.S. 574 (1983).

10. Afterword
Richard John Neuhaus
1. See above, Chaper 7, 149.
2. St. Augustine De Trinitate 1, 5.

About the Contributors

GERARD V. BRADLEY is professor of law at the University of Notre Dame Law School. He is also the director, with John Finnis, of Notre Dame's Natural Law Institute. A noted scholar in the areas of constitutional law and church and state issues, he has recently served as president of the Fellowship of Catholic Scholars, as a member of the board of advisors of the Cardinal Newman Society, and as chair of the Federalist Society's Religious Liberties Practice Group. He is the author of *A Student's Guide to the Study of Law* (2006), and *Essays on Law and Morality* (2009).

MARY ANN GLENDON is the Learned Hand Professor of Law at Harvard University, and former U.S. Ambassador to the Holy See. She writes and teaches in the fields of human rights, comparative law, constitutional law, and legal theory. Her books include *A Nation Under Lawyers* (1996); *A World Made New: Eleanor Roosevelt and the Universal Declaration of Human Rights* (2001); and *Traditions in Turmoil* (2006).

J. H. H. WEILER is Joseph Straus Professor of Law and Director of the Hauser Global Law School Program at New York University. Previously, he taught at the University of Michigan Law School and Harvard Law School. A fellow of the American Academy of

Arts and Sciences, he holds honorary professorships at University College, London, and the University of Copenhagen. He is the author of *The EU, the WTO, and the NAFTA: Towards a Common Law of International Trade?* (2000) and *The European Court of Justice,* edited with Grainne de Burca (2001).

MICHAEL PAKALUK is professor of philosophy at the Institute for the Psychological Sciences in Arlington, Virginia, and visiting associate professor of philosophy at the Catholic University of America. He has published extensively in the history of philosophy and in political philosophy, covering topics related to Aristotle, Plato, Aquinas, Hume, and Reid. He is the author of *Other Selves: Philosophers on Friendship* (1991); the Clarendon Aristotle volume on Books VIII and IX of the *Nicomachean Ethics* (1998); and *Aristotle's Nicomachean Ethics: An Introduction* (2005).

JOHN FINNIS has taught jurisprudence at University College, Oxford since 1966, and is professor of law and legal philosophy at the University of Oxford. He has also taught at University of Adelaide, the University of Malawi, Boston College, and the University of Notre Dame where he is Biolchini Family Professor of Law. A Fellow of the British Academy, his books include *Natural Law and Natural Rights* (1980); *Fundamentals of Ethics* (1983); *Nuclear Deterrence, Morality, and Realism* (1987); *Moral Absolutes* (1991); and *Aquinas: Moral, Political, and Legal Theory* (1998).

ROGERS M. SMITH is the Christopher H. Browne Distinguished Professor of Political Science at the University of Pennsylvania and Chair of the Penn Program on Democracy, Citizenship, and Constitutionalism. His books include *Civic Ideals: Conflicting Visions of Citizenship in U.S. History* (1997) and *Stories of Peoplehood: The Politics and Morals of Political Memberships* (2003). In 2004, he was elected a Fellow of the American Academy of Arts and Sciences.

Eric Gregory is Assistant Professor of Religion at Princeton University. He is the author of *Politics & the Order of Love: An Augustinian Ethic of Democratic Citizenship* (2008), and various articles on religion and ethics, including "Before the Original Position: The Neo-Orthodox Theology of the Young John Rawls" (*Journal of Religious Ethics,* 2007). A graduate of Harvard College, he did graduate studies in theology as a Rhodes Scholar at Oxford and received his doctorate in religious studies from Yale University. In 2007, he was awarded Princeton's President's Award for Distinguished Teaching.

William A. Galston is Senior Fellow and Ezra Zilkha Chair in Governance Studies at the Brookings Institution. During the first Clinton Administration, he served as Deputy Assistant to the President for Domestic Policy and later as executive director for the National Commission on Civic Renewal, co-chaired by William Bennett and Sam Nunn. He taught for seventeen years at the Maryland School of Public Policy, where he served as professor, dean, director of the Institute for Philosophy and Public Policy at the University of Maryland, and founding director of the Center for Information and Research on Civic Learning and Engagement (CIRCLE). He is the author of eight books, most recently *Public Matters: Politics, Policy, and Religion in the 21st Century* (2005).

Hadley Arkes is the Edward N. Ney Professor in American Institutions at Amherst College, where he has been a member of the faculty since 1966. He was the primary architect of the Born Alive Infant's Protection Act, signed in 2002. He has served as visiting professor of public and international affairs at the Woodrow Wilson School, and as the Vaughan Fellow at the James Madison Program at Princeton University. He is the author of *The Philosopher in the City* (1981), *First Things* (1986), *Beyond the Constitution* (1990), and *Natural Rights and the Right to Choose* (2002).

RICHARD JOHN NEUHAUS (1936–2009) was the founding editor of *First Things* and the director of the Institute on Religion and Public Life. Converting from Lutheranism to Roman Catholicism in 1990, Father Neuhaus was ordained a priest in the Roman Catholic Church in 1991. An outspoken advocate of pro-life causes, he was a close, unofficial advisor to President George W. Bush and a key figure in many ecumenical efforts, such as the publication, with Charles Colson, of *Evangelicals and Catholics Together: Toward a Common Mission* (1995). His books include *The Naked Public Square: Religion and Democracy in America* (1984); *The Catholic Moment* (1987); *Death on a Friday Afternoon* (2001); and *Catholic Matters: Confusion, Controversy, and the Splendor of Truth* (2007).

Index

About the Editor

Christopher Wolfe is emeritus professor of political science at Marquette University and the author or editor of numerous books and articles, including *The Rise of Modern Judicial Review*, *How to Read the Constitution*, *Natural Law and Public Reason*, and *Natural Law Liberalism*. He is the founder and president of the American Public Philosophy Institute, vice president of the Thomas International Project, and co-director of the Ralph McInerny Center for Thomistic Studies.